THE SOU

THE SOUL OF ISLAM

ESSENTIAL DOCTRINES AND BELIEFS

TWO TREATISES BY
SHAYKH MUHAMMAD EMIN ER

TRANSLATED BY JOSEPH WALSH

AL-MADINA
INSTITUTE

The Soul of Islam
© Copyright: Al Madina Institute 2014
ISBN: 978-0-9900026-5-9
Published by: Al Madina Institute
www.almadinainstitute.org

Author: Shaykh Muhammad Emin Er
Translated by Joseph Walsh
Editors: Tamin Azaibi & Kashif Munir
Design and Typsetting: Abdallateef Whiteman
Printed in the United States of America

CONTENTS

O visitor to me, traveling through the ever-fading world,
Be certain that the path is perilous, so follow Muhammad!
If you do, you shall be beloved, forgiven, and saved by his
Generous Master, And be with Allah's beloved for ever
and in eternity, in the Abode of Permanence!

SHAYKH MUHAMMAD EMIN ER

PART I

Introducing Shaykh Muhammad Emin Er

THE BOOK YOU now hold in your hands collects the basic writings of the last true religious scholar of the Ottoman world, translated for the first time into English.

The late Shaykh Muhammed Emin Er was a traditionally educated scholar of the sacred sciences of Islam. In the present day, many of us are scarcely aware of the full significance of a life of scholarship as understood by Muslims for nearly a millennium and a half, let alone how to esteem such a person as a link in a living chain connecting us to the last of God's Messengers, Muhammad, may God bless him and grant him peace. Where once these chains of transmission were numerous, today few persist. The writings collected here preserve the learning that these chains represent in their written aspect, just as the author himself preserved and exemplified its living, unwritten dimension.

Many Muslims – indeed, many believers within every faith – argue endlessly among themselves concerning the proper balance of the inner, "spiritual" life with the outer, "religious" life. In the present day, many of us are scarcely aware that the question of a possible contradiction between these is as new as it is baseless. Consistent with the opinions of the greatest

I

scholars of the earlier generations of Islam, Shaykh Emin holds that the inner and outer aspects of a life spent in the service of God logically require and reciprocally complement each other. Any barrier that we might place between them is not only artificial, but proposes a departure from the authentic normative tradition of Islam. Much of what is written here demonstrates how and why this must be so.

According to Shaykh Emin, a purely legalistic understanding of religion – Islam without spirituality, or law without love – is an unwarranted novelty, one to be rejected on the grounds that it was not the way of the Prophet Muhammad, may God bless him and grant him peace, or of his Companions, may God be pleased with them all. And he holds it to be true that a purely spiritual interpretation of Islam, devoid of the legal and moral norms brought by the Prophet and his Companions, is equally a novelty, lacking in a solid foundation and detrimental to a life lived in selfless service to the Most High. The governing principle of the life and teaching of Shaykh Emin can be best summarized *as commitment to the best conduct and highest courtesy possible towards God and His creation.* This conduct and courtesy emerge naturally and organically from a life of scholarship and pious and humble practice, motivated solely by sincere love of God Most High. As the texts presented here will show, Shaykh Emin concerns himself not with knowledge *about* religion, but knowledge *of* religion. This distinction is vital, since it captures a key difference between (respectively) modern and traditional approaches to religious practice and spiritual growth.

The highest tradition of Ottoman religious education espoused the essential unity of knowledge of the inner and outer aspects of religion, spiritual psychology (*tasawwuf*), and sacred law (*sharīʿa*). This enabled each scholar to become a living exemplar of a humanistic, compassionate, and inclusive Islam that is the fruit not of the "religion-building" efforts of progressives and reformers now much in vogue, but of the integral, rigorous, and yet flexible practice of Islam as it was known to generations past. Shaykh Emin is one of the last – if not the very last – of the scholars of this type, capable of connecting seekers in the 21st century to this long and still-vital tradition. Thus both Muslims and non-Muslims have much to gain from an acquaintance with the general contours of his teaching, which we will now summarize.

There can be little question that the fruits of traditional Islamic life and thought bear little resemblance to those typical of modernist movements within Islam, such as Salafism and Wahhabism. The Ottoman world was uniquely pluricultural, yet held together through a kind of universalism that Shaykh Emin embodies in perspectives like the following:

God has commanded us to believe that we are always in the midst of people who are spiritually pure, highly regarded by Him, and precious to Him. This thought prevents us from indulging ourselves in evil thoughts and shameful, illicit conduct. If we believe ourselves to be constantly among spiritually pure and precious people, we are prevented from pursuing evil ends and acting in ways that God has forbidden.

That such an outlook might seem to be atypical among contemporary Muslims shows how much work remains to be done towards spiritual and religious renewal, and how much is still squandered on politics. And it would be wrong to imagine that this is an attitude no longer relevant to contemporary societies. Shaykh Emin's commitment to reviving the changeless core of Islamic knowledge takes full stock of the changing conditions of humanity, aiming to make traditional Islamic knowledge more readily and directly applicable to contemporary circumstances, as well as more readily accessible to the current generation of sincere spiritual seekers. His life-long project can be characterized as striving to help more people benefit from the fruits of the Islamic scholarly tradition, as well as to increase its benefits to those who already embrace it.

Toward this end, Shaykh Emin has made his primary focus the axiomatic principles or *darūriyyāt*, which is to say, those areas of knowledge and scholarship that are obligatory for all believers. For instance, knowledge of God is the highest priority for a student, because all believers must acquire this before delving into knowledge of other sorts. This enables us to comprehend our nature as creatures [*makhlūq*] in relation to the divine Creator [*al-Khāliq*], our nature as servants of God [*ʿabīd*] obliged to devote ourselves to His worship [*ʿibāda*]. The other branches of religious knowledge, such as law or linguistics, are secondary to the *darūriyyāt* in that not all believers are obliged to pursue them. Certainly all Muslims are encouraged to approach these subjects, but it suffices for a group of specialists to assume their study in depth as fulfillment of the obligation to seek knowledge that devolves to a community rather than to every individual within it.

As a living link within an *isnād*, that is, within an unbroken lineage of transmission of knowledge extending back to the Prophet Muhammad, may God bless him and grant him peace, Shaykh Emin places utmost emphasis on the necessity of internalizing the example [*sunna*] of the Prophet, exemplifying it both in one's physical actions and one's spiritual states. To accomplish this, only direct transmission within an *isnād* will do – books alone can never suffice and, once broken, neither an authentic chain of transmission nor the living reality of the prophetic *sunna* in our midst can again be fully realized. Shaykh Emin teaches that one who knows the *sunna* of the Prophet, may God bless him and grant him peace, is to act upon it, and one who does not know this *sunna* is to seek it by following those who do.

Shaykh Emin also teaches that the scholar who has reached the level of direct, personal derivation of Islamic norms from their sources (a process known as *ijtihād*) is free to draw his understanding of Islam directly from the Qur'ān and *hadīth*. And by the same token, those who have not attained this level must learn it from the *mujtahid* scholars, that is, those very few for whom *ijtihād* is permitted. In the present day, the genuine background and capacity for *ijtihād* is as rare as the pretense to it is widespread. Shaykh Emin proposes that one cure for this disorder among Muslims whose main source of knowledge must be through books is to read only the books of the *mujtahid* scholars, since the writings of others carry no weight in Islamic law.

Particularly significant is Shaykh Emin's understanding of the relation of the inner and outer dimensions of Islam, that is, of spiritual psychology to the sacred law. In his view, the law comprises two dimensions, called ʿazīma and rukhsa. The latter, rukhsa, means roughly *dispensation*, and alludes to the law in its most flexible and lenient aspect. Muslims are free to meet their religious obligations in multiple ways, including ways approved by the scholars that are nevertheless accommodating to personal circumstances and limitations. The approach through rukhsa depends upon the existence of differences among scholarly opinion concerning acceptable means for fulfilling religious obligations, such that one is able to choose the path that is both valid and convenient in the face of a particular constraint. It is not always appreciated by contemporary Muslims, who typically have too little access to sound religious education, that the law is characterized above all by its leniency, as shown through a range of equally acceptable alternatives in religious practice not attested in any other faith tradition.

As the complement of the way of rukhsa, ʿazīma refers to *strictness* or *rigor*, by which is meant the manner of fulfilling requirements of the revealed law that emphasizes scholarly consensus among those who are properly considered to be *mujtahid*. Accordingly, one does not seek ease or accommodation, but only the means of fulfilling one's duties with the least latitude in scholarly opinion. What course of action, in other words, would be satisfying to the legal theories of *every* qualified scholar? What approach would meet the stipulations, if at all possible, of the *mujtahid* scholars of every normative school of legal interpretation, be it Hanafi, Hanbali, Maliki, or Shafii?

Shaykh Emin holds that the way of ʿ*azīma* is effectively synonymous with the way of Islamic spirituality, that is, of *tasawwuf*. Furthermore, ʿ*azīma* in this understanding is identical to the *sunna* of the Prophet, may God bless him and grant him peace. Thus, the way of *tasawwuf* is quite literally and simply *kamāl iʿtizām as-sunna*, which is to say the complete embodiment in one's actions, speech, and relations to the most rigorous model [ʿ*azīma*] of the *sunna*. This standard is not to be imposed on others, who may have very good reasons for seeking accommodation through *rukhsa*, but it can be embraced voluntarily by the energetic seeker, through the way of *tasawwuf*.

It is remarkable that this *sunna* is considered by Shaykh Emin to be, in effect, not that of the Prophet Muhammad alone, may God bless him and grant him peace, but that of *all* previous prophets. Quite simply, the *sunna* of Muhammad, may God bless him and grant him peace, includes that of Jesus and Moses, peace be upon them both, as well as of all the other prophets.

Thus it is by no means the case that the paths inherited by the followers of these respective prophets, and embodied in different faith traditions, are in any way mutually incompatible. And it logically follows that the practice of *tasawwuf* through *kamāl iʿtizām as-sunna* fully encompasses the practice of the way of Jesus, of Moses, and so forth, peace be upon them all.

It should go without saying that this perspective

affords a striking and welcome opening not only to a fulfilling spirituality within Islam, but to new horizons in interfaith dialogue as well. The Muslim who embodies ʿazīma – the person of tasawwuf – is the living exemplar of the highest ideals of Judaism, Christianity, and Islam. To those who might ask, "What would Jesus do?" Shaykh Emin has a very good answer.

For Shaykh Emin, the history of divine interaction with humankind through the prophets has been one of instructing communities of belief in particular methods of worship. Each prophet receives not only a particular model prescribed for a given historical community, but represents the embodiment of particular virtues, such as courage or generosity. In the Qurʾān one readily observes that, after the mention of each of their examples, the Prophet Muhammad, may God bless him and grant him peace, is commanded to follow their way. Thus both the examples and the virtues of all the prophets are gathered in the example and character of the last of the prophets, may God bless him and grant him peace. And these are conferred as well upon his community.

This being so, there can be no possibility of conflict between the people of tasawwuf and those of the communities of earlier prophets.

What is more, the community of Muhammad, may God bless him and grant him peace, has been distinguished by the completion of the means of worship given by God Most High to His angels. Some of the angels are created by the Most High in the position of qiyām (the posture that opens the ritual prayer [salāt]), standing in this way for untold thousands of years without food, drink, or respite.

Some angels have remained in the bowing position of the prayer (*rukū'*), never once raising their heads since they were created; and others likewise have remained in prostration (*sujūd*).

Only the community of the Last Prophet, may God bless him and grant him peace, has been graced with the command that all of these motions be joined in the ritual prayer. This fact is reflected in the letters of the name of the first of the prophets, Adam, peace be upon him. Thus the *alif*, the vertical stroke representing the first letter of Adam's name, corresponds to the standing position; the *dāl*, or second letter, to the bowing; and the *mīm* to the final letter of the name and the final motion of *salāt*, the prostration. So the community of Muhammad, may God bless him and grant him peace, is graced not only with the fulfillment of the *sunna* of all the previous prophets, but of that of the angels as well. And in this is found the real significance of the goal of spiritual practice, of *kamāl i'tizām as-sunna*.

Shaykh Emin teaches that there are five requirements for spiritual progress, ranked as follows:

+ *khidma*, which is service to the Truth (*al-Haqq*, one of the Names of God) and to creation as a whole

+ *muhabba*, which is love for God, for His creation, and above all for one's master and companions in the spiritual path

+ *sohba*, spiritual friendship and mutually supportive interaction and conversation among brothers and sisters in the path of seeking

• *al-ʿamal bi-mā huwa'l-awlā fī'l-waqt*, the practice of that action which is most appropriate to the moment – that is, which is foremost in virtue in a given circumstance

• *dhikr*, the remembrance of God at all times and without exception, bearing in mind that He sees us even if we do not see Him

It is striking that service to others is placed before all else in order of priority, while *dhikr* appears at the end of this list of the prerequisites for spiritual progress. This view arises from the understanding that "transitive" acts of worship – that is, those having an object among created entities – are superior to "intransitive" acts of worship lacking such an object. Service to others is transitive; contemplation in a secluded place is intransitive. Likewise, to remain in Mecca and circumambulate the Kaʿba every day is intransitive, however praiseworthy; circling the world to teach others their religion is both transitive and preferable.

All of this implies a great deal of love and concern for others, and to be sure, Shaykh Emin espouses this towards all, Muslim and non-Muslim alike. He considers all people to be his children, all of us to be his brothers and sisters.

According to Shaykh Emin, there are three levels of brotherhood. First, there is a level of brotherhood emergent in our common heritage as children of Adam, peace be upon him. Brotherhood of this sort is obtained regardless of anyone's faith commitment, religious identity, or acquired or hereditary qualities. Next is the level of brotherhood among Muslims in a shared faith, emergent from the sharing of particular practices and beliefs that impart a common worldview and way of life. And last is the level of brotherhood appropriate to those who share in their striving in the path of knowledge, spiritual growth, and dedication to the service of God and His creation.

This being so, service to humanity might properly be seen as the pivotal principle of Shaykh Emin's teaching. This principle is grounded in wishing for others what one wishes for oneself, in particular in the areas of knowledge and moral guidance responsible for prosperity and happiness in this world and salvation in the Hereafter. Echoes here of the Golden Rule of the Gospels ought not to be surprising, given earlier remarks concerning the people of *tasawwuf* as exemplars of the *sunna* of Jesus, peace be upon him.

And it is not only other Muslims that Muslims are charged to serve, not only the rights of other Muslims that Muslims are required to protect. Whereas God Most High might well forgive one of us for transgressing His rights, it is less certain that we will receive pardon for offenses against the rights of our human brothers and sisters, our fellow descendants of the Prophet Adam, peace be upon him.

Although not routinely observed among Muslims today, it is nevertheless an accepted principle in Islam that one is to seek the pardon of the person one has offended, offering full compensation for harms done and seeking reconciliation with one's brothers and sisters *before* seeking the pardon of God. Consequently, Muslims are to regard offenses against our non-Muslim fellows as particularly risky – what, after all, might motivate the non-Muslim to forgive the Muslim, especially on the Day of Judgment? To be sure, Muslims are supposed to understand the merit of forgiving their coreligionists, and fully expect to receive the rewards of the Hereafter attendant upon this pardon and forbearance. But what of the non-Muslim who, having little or no belief in God or the next life, sees no reason to forgive? According to this perspective, the duty to protect the rights and respect the concerns of non-Muslims weighs especially heavily upon the Muslim who believes fervently in God and the Last Day.

Similarly, Muslims must take special care as custodians of all in God's creation that is not human. We cannot communicate with animals to implore their forgiveness, though animals have rights against which human beings can and do transgress. The same is true of other animate and even inanimate beings. The Qur'ān and *hadīth* teach that animals, plants, and even stones are sentient in their own ways, that they worship God in their own ways, and thus that they have rights over us in their own ways. How are we to compensate such beings for the harms we do, let alone seek their pardon before God Most High?

Asked about his understanding of the meaning of the word *Islam* by a European visitor, Shaykh Emin had this to say:

> In Arabic, the word islām means to surrender to God. That is why Islam is not only the religion of the followers of Muhammad, may God bless him and grant him peace, whom we call Muslims, but of all people living on this earth. That is because this religion called Islam was not

sent only to Muslims, but to all the people of the world. All of the other prophets were sent to transmit the message of God to the people.

Everything – even the stones, and this plant, and all the animals – are in a state of surrender to God. All things are organized according to God's determination, and live under a law prescribed by God. And so these entities offer no resistance, show no disobedience to God. Even our hands, our eyes, our bodies do not disobey God, but perform their duties according to a natural law. Which is why we also, as people, must come to obey the commands of God.

We are in no position to question God, but we are very much in a position for God to question us. Islam means complete surrender at any cost, and so it is not for us to ask why some people are rich, why some are clever, why some are healthy, why we are not rich, why we do not receive more money, why we are not powerful. It is not for us to ask such questions. We will be questioned by God, and without complete surrender to God's determining we will not have proved ourselves to be fully His servants, as His law has prescribed for us.

In our religion we also do not complain when we suffer pain, but are instead submissive before what God has decreed for us. This is because pain is of three types. The first type is punishment for our sins. The second type is to redeem us of these sins. And the third type is to raise us in our stature before God. We believe that, in every case, what comes to us is only from God, and that we are obligated to practice patience and to pray only to Him in our distress. We are also cognizant of the fact that the greatest suffering is directed by God to those whom He most loves, such as the prophets. So we pray to Him that our suffering will be a way to overcome sins and face Him free of sin in the life to come.

+ + +

Muhammad Emin Er was born near the outbreak of World War I, possibly in 1914. The official records of the time are not always trustworthy, such that the exact date of his birth is uncertain. His birthplace was the village of Külüyan (recently renamed Kalaş), near the town of Çermik, province of Diyarbakır, in the southeast of what is now Turkey but was at that time the Ottoman Empire.

Shaykh Emin's family belonged to a Kurdish tribe called Mīrān[1]. His father, Haji Zülfikar (commonly known as Zülfügül), was a farmer who took a great interest in science and education, and happened to be a person of some wealth. There being no school in the village of Külüyan, Haji Zülfikar employed a private tutor to educate his two young sons, Muhammad Emin and his elder brother, Ali. In addition to paying the tutor's salary and expenses, Haji Zülfikar assisted him in finding a wife and establishing a family in the village. He also gave him a gift of land, specifically the garden where Haji Zülfikar's family had traditionally grown vegetables to meet its own needs. Then, just as his sons were learning to read and write in the Arabic script (at the time still the official script of the Ottoman language and state), Haji Zülfikar passed away. The future Shaykh had already lost his mother

Havvā while he was still a young child of the age of three or four, and thus (like the Prophet Muhammad, may God bless him and grant him peace) he was left an orphan.

(Till his death, Shaykh Emin traveled to the graves of his mother and father in the village of Külüyan at least once per year. As Muslims always have, he greeted the deceased in their graves, and they reply, pleased to have received his visit.)

At this time, Muhammad Emin was 10 years old, and the Ottoman state still stood as one of the largest in the world, extending from North Africa to Yemen, and from the Balkans to the frontiers of Persia. It faced coordinated attacks on many fronts, east and west. The Allied Powers, which for many years had sought to subvert and undermine Ottoman autonomy indirectly, now set out to defeat it directly by force and to invade its vast and wealthy lands. Because of the war, the economic situation became ruinous, as the Ottoman state was increasingly forced to deplete its already overextended financial resources in the defense of its territorial integrity. The resulting economic hardship was severe throughout the country, and not least in the impoverished regions of Eastern Anatolia where Shaykh Emin grew up.

The young Muhammad Emin passed through the remainder of his early life in much straightened circumstances, first under the care of his stepmother, and later under that of his elder brother. He contributed to the support of his family by sheperding goats in the high mountains surrounding the village. All the while, his desire to learn to read and write, ignited both by his late father and his former tutor, persisted

and grew. Having neither paper nor pen, he used stones to scratch words and sentences on flat rocks while
tending his goats on the mountainsides. This striving
to improve his reading and writing skills despite great
deprivation gave rise to the legend in his village that
Khidr, the companion of Moses and saintly figure
who comes to the aid of the destitute, provided the
young Muhammad Emin lessons in his sleep.

So great was the young child's passion for knowledge
that he would cry bitter tears while imploring God
to help him learn to read the Qur'ān. He missed no
opportunity to seek out people who he thought might
help him. He would journey on foot for several days
at a time simply to visit knowledgeable people in the
vicinity of his village, however briefly. At length he
learned how to write letters and read books in the
Ottoman script.

As for the Arabic language and knowledge of the
traditional Islamic disciplines, there was at the time
no one in the region able to introduce him to this type
of scholarship. Thus he sought what knowledge he
could from books. One of the first books he read was
Tezkiyetunnufus by Eşrefoğlu Rumi, where the author
listed the qualities of a reliable master of the inner
path[2]. Muhammad Emin sought out these qualities in
the few scholars he was able to visit.

In due course, the war came to an end. The traditional Ottoman script was abolished by the nacent
Turkish Republic, its use outlawed together with all
Qur'ānic and Islamic education. Families began to
fear the consequences of teaching the Qur'ān to their
children even in the privacy of their own homes.

As Shaykh Emin recalls today, the first awakenings

of his spiritual quest came to him very early, but there were few options open to him:

> From my early childhood I was anxious with respect to death and the life to come, so I would visit certain teachers and inquire with them about all this. I asked them how to prepare myself for the next life. From early childhood I was curious about such things. I kept asking older people why we are so interested in this life and the things of this world, when we are going to die, absolutely every one of us. So it became my main goal to seek out a teacher and gain a religious education.
>
> But at that time everything was forbidden in Turkey. Even to read and to learn the Qur'ān was forbidden in those days. It was not easy, like it is today. We had very hard times, so I resolved at my first opportunity to seek religious learning in Syria.

This was not to be. Reaching the border city of Gaziantep, Muhammad Emin was not permitted to cross into Syria. He resolved instead to travel first to Adana, and soon thereafter to Istanbul. Knowing no one in Istanbul, he soon ran out of money, and thus went on foot to Bursa where he worked as a servant for a wealthy family in order to make a living. Eventually he returned to Adana. Here, having travelled for seven years, he saw Khidr in a dream, and was instructed to visit his relatives in his hometown. He accordingly returned to Külüyan for a period of time.

At the age of twenty-five, Muhammad Emin made his first of many trips of pilgrimage [*hajj*] to the Sacred

House, in Mecca. Upon his return, his desire to seek sacred knowledge undiminished, he undertook extensive travels in eastern Anatolia to seek out scholars and ask them to teach him. His first teacher was Molla Hasan Tahvīkī, the Mufti of Derik, a town in the region of Mardin. Molla Hasan taught him *sarf*, or linguistic morphology, the fundamental science of the inflection of Arabic words. Next he travelled to the town of Garza in the region of Siirt, where he studied Arabic syntax (*nahw*) under Molla Rasul. While in Garza he also studied advanced topics in *sarf* and *nahw* with Molla Abdurrasul.

At length he resolved once again to cross into Syria in search of scholars who could instruct him. By now World War II had begun, and although he succeeded in crossing the border, he was detained by security forces who suspected him of being a spy. He spent some time in prison in Syria before being cleared. Set free by the authorities, he returned to Turkey, in particular to Diyarbakır. Here he was able to study the remaining subjects in the foundational curriculum of the traditional Islamic sciences, many of them concerned with Arabic linguistics. These included logic (*mantiq*), historical semantics (*ʿilm al-wadʿ*), figurative usage (*istiʿāra*), prose style (*adab*), lexicology (*maʿānin*), rhetoric (*bayān*), refined usage (*badīʿ*), fundamentals of religious belief and practice (*usūl ad-dīn*), and theoretical jurisprudence (*usūl al-fiqh*).

The teacher with whom he spent the greatest part of this time was Molla Rasul, who was originally from Van but had relocated to Diyarbakır. Molla Rasul was a classmate of the famous Bediüzzaman Said Nursi, and used to mention him frequently. In Diyarbakır,

Shaykh Emin also studied advanced topics in *sarf* and *nahw* with Molla Abdulhalim. He learned other important points in *nahw* from Molla Shaykh Aburrezzak, a great scholar and Sufi master, who lived in the village of Halili in Mardin.

Molla Hafiz Haci Haydar Efendi and Molla Shaykh Zeynelabidin were Shaykh Emin's teachers in the sciences of Qur'ānic recitation, *makhārij al-hurūf* and *tajwīd*. The latter of these teachers lived in the village of Fursa, near the town of Tillo in the district of Siirt. Here Shaykh Emin learned Islamic theology (*kalām*) from Molla Shaykh Sherefuddin Fursavī. He also studied briefly with Shaykh Ahmad Shorshubi, from the village of Shorshub in Diyarbakır, who used to give lessons while sitting on his knees although he was more than eighty years old. Because the *madrasa* of this scholar was so crowded, Shaykh could not remain there for very long.

In 1951, Shaykh Emin completed the last of his studies, completing the study of *kalām* with Molla Shaykh Muhammad Ma'shuk³. This was the teacher who conferred upon Muhammad Emin his *ijāza* (the traditional diploma and authorization to teach) in all of the rational sciences and traditional Islamic disciplines which have constituted the curriculum of the great scholars of the Islamic tradition since the time of Imām Ghazālī in the 11th-12th centuries CE. In addition to those already mentioned, Shaykh Emin mastered and received *ijāza* in the sciences of Islamic jurisprudence (*fiqh*), exegesis of Qur'ān (*tafsīr*), religious laws of inheritance (*farā'id*), and the sciences of the prophetic traditions (*usūl al-hadīth*).

Concurrent with these studies in the rational sciences, Shaykh Emin also pursued knowledge of *tasawwuf*, the normative discipline of spiritual psychology characteristic of Islam. He had three principal mentors in what can also be called the Sufi path, all from the Naqshibandi order.

His first mentor in the path was Shaykh Ahmad Khaznawi, from Khazna in Syria, whom he met while he was in Syria. Following the death of Shaykh Ahmad, he was re-initiated to the Sufi way by Shaykh Muhammad Saʿīd Saydā al-Jazarī (known affectionately as Saydā), from Cizre in Diyarbakır, and remained under his discipline until he was given *ijāza* to train disciples of his own. When Shaykh Saʿīd Saydā al-Jazarī passed away, Shaykh Emin was affiliated with Shaykh Muhammad Samin of Istanbul, until the latter died.

Shaykh Emin first met Shaykh Saydā after the death of Shaykh Khaznawi. Shaykh recalls that he had heard Saydā's name from others who had studied with him or entered his devotional lineage [*tarīqa*], including two teachers of his own. At the time, the successor [*khalīfa*] of Shaykh Khaznawi was still alive, and thus Shaykh Emin was initially hesitant to seek out Shaykh Saydā instead. However, a combination of dreams and indications obtained through a special prayer of consultation [*istikhara*] culminated for him in Ramadan of that year. This led him to travel to Cizre and report his experiences to Saydā directly. Based upon the interpretation of these experiences, Shaykh Emin at last entered the *tarīqa* of Shaykh Saydā. It was from Shaykh Saʿīd Saydā al-Jazarī that Shaykh Emin received his most formative training, and his permission to teach in the Naqshibandi lineage.

Saydā established a place of retreat in his house, in effect a sort of cave called a *çilehane* or "house of ordeal". For us, such a tiny and constricting place would be at best boring, if not fearfully claustrophobic – and all too often, we flee from such places and experiences to the distractions of human company. Yet for Saydā, this *çilehane* was a place of spiritual education and intimacy with God Most High. For a teacher of Saydā's high spiritual station [*maqām*], to spend time among ordinary, heedless people could only be considered an ordeal, albeit one incumbent upon him in emulation of the practice of the Prophet, may God bless him and grant him peace, who returned to his community from his Night Journey to his Lord.

Such patience from one of so high a spiritual level, together with complete commitment to the norms of the sacred law and the *sunna* of the Prophet, may God bless him and grant him peace, are all criteria for recognizing genuine teachers in the tradition of this path. The teacher marked by what is called in Persian *hubbu jāh*, love of the crowd, betrays through this that he is not a real teacher. How, after all, can the companionship of creatures such as ourselves ever be preferable to that of the Creator of us all?

Shaykh Emin teaches that among genuine teachers, one recognizes two types, distinguished according to their preparation and ability to instruct others. The first of these is *irshādī*, which is to say a teacher who has acquired his training and who functions among his students at the level of discourse. (The word *irshādī* comes from an Arabic root whose meaning refers to guidance.) His experience of the path is derived from books and pious conversation, and it is on this basis that he is able to counsel others.

Granting that the use of reason is necessary for progress in the path, it certainly cannot be regarded as sufficient. This idea is famously asserted by Imām Ghazālī in one of his principle works[4], where he expresses concern over the degree to which even correct and substantial rational proofs leave room for perilous uncertainty – one rational proof sufficing to undo the knowledge obtained by a different one. In contrast, he writes of the people of *tasawwuf* that:

> their most distinctive characteristic is something that can be attained, not by study, but rather by fruitional experience [*dhawq*] and the state of ecstasy [*ḥāl*] and the exchange of qualities [*tabaddul as-sifāt*]. How great a difference there is between your *knowing* the definition and causes and conditions of health and satiety and your *being* healthy and sated! [...] [W]hen a physician is ill, he knows the definition and causes of health and the remedies which procure it, though he is then actually bereft of health. Similarly too, there is a difference between your knowing the true nature and conditions and causes of asceticism and your actually practicing asceticism and personally shunning the things of this world.

> I knew with certainty that the sufis were masters of states, not purveyors of words, and that I had learned all I could by way of theory. There remained, then, only what was attainable, not by hearing and study, but by fruitional experience and actually engaging in the way. From the

sciences which I had practiced and the methods which I had followed in my inquiry into the two kinds of knowledge, revealed and rational, I had already acquired a sure and certain faith in God Most High, in the prophetic mediation of revelation, and in the Last Day. These three fundamentals of our Faith had become deeply rooted in my soul, not because of any specific, precisely formulated proofs, but because of reasons and circumstances and experiences too many to list in detail.

The second type of teacher is *tasarruf*, one who operates not only through the mind or through rational training, but who indeed can transform others through direct interaction with the heart. (The root meaning of the word *tasarruf* concerns transformation.) Such a teacher also emphasizes *sohba*, the emulation of the *sunna* of the Prophet, may God bless him and grant him peace, with his Companions, may God be pleased with them all, according to which pious discourses and mutual consultation in a context of true brotherhood inspire and guide the heart[5].

It is to this second category that Saydā and Shaykh Emin both belong. The *tasarruf* teacher has reached his level through spiritual wayfaring, cleansing of the subtle centers[6] called the *latā'if*, and reception of *kashf*, or the unveiling of divine secrets directly to the heart rather than the mind. For this type of teacher rationality has its place, but is not primary – and certainly the experiences of the mind are no substitute for intimate presence with God Most High.

As already mentioned, a cornerstone of Saydā's

method of instructing his students in the path was the practice of *sohba*. Shaykh Emin always held that every lineage has its own methods of remembrance [*dhikr*] and other practices, but that among all of them, the practice of *sohba* is particularly indispensable and uniquely effective. Those educated without it cannot reach the level of the *tasarruf* teacher, capable of serving as a guide to other people[7]. This is shown by the fact that those people who, in their lifetimes, experienced *sohba* with the Prophet, may God bless him and grant him peace, are far higher in spiritual degree and righteous stature than those who did not.

Consistent with the true spirit and aims of *sohba*, Saydā's love for his students was very great, and was coupled with tremendous humility. He would brush flies from the faces of his students as they spoke, and kiss their shoes to obtain their forgiveness of others for slights and disputes. He would travel to the homes his students to teach them (a high and uncommon courtesy within his culture), or address crowds that had questions for him, answering all with boundless patience. Shaykh Emin continued these practices in his own life.

Shaykh Emin recalled in particular an occasion when Ramadan fell during the summer, and Shaykh Saydā had ridden (as was his wont during Ramadan) to an outlying village to provide the people with instruction and guidance. Believing his teaching was finished for the time being, Saydā began to mount his donkey in the blazing heat of midday when one further question was put to him. In spite of the discomfort imposed by his fast, Saydā remained in that place debating and discussing with people until all were satisfied, and only then rode on to seek rest and shade.

In the spirit of concealing the faults of people, Saydā accepted every excuse, from students or others, without question. This was true even when he knew people plainly to be lying to him in order to cover up for themselves. Shaykh Emin recalls an occasion when two of Saydā's students were discussing the consequences of arriving late for their lesson. One student was apprehensive, but the other insisted that there was no cause for concern, that Saydā would himself invent some excuse on their behalf. And this he did.

No one ever heard Saydā utter a harsh or disparaging word against any other person, nor did he defend himself against such talk by others. Indeed, when he caught wind of the slander of others directed against him, Saydā's only response would be to aver that *I have more faults than they know*. Saydā inspired right conduct in those around him not by talk, but by his own example. On one occasion he learned of two brothers in his village who were building a house but did not have enough stone to complete the job. Though quite elderly by this time, Saydā went to a ruined house and asked his students to place two stones from it on his back so that he could carry them to the house being constructed. This led many others to participate in the work of mutual support and assistance so integral to the practice of *sohba*.

Saydā would offer his mount to scholars he met on his rounds who happened to be traveling on foot, with the same beneficial incentive to universal generosity. On one occasion when traveling from village to village with a crowd that may have included a thousand people, the leading religious authority [*muftī*] of the region begged leave to depart from this company in order to return to his duties in the city. Because surrendering one's horse to the *muftī* would have meant being unable to keep up with Saydā's party as it traveled, none present could be persuaded to make this offer. Once Saydā gave up his own donkey, however, a great many of those accompanying him were inspired to emulate his gesture by giving up their own.

Indeed, Saydā had a donkey to offer on this occasion because he would consent to ride only donkeys, never horses. This was due to his concern for preserving his humility. He refused to accept a horse as his mount even when it was offered, and even when his companions were themselves on horseback. On one occasion when his donkey abandoned him in a neighboring village to walk back home without him, Saydā refused to ride home on a horse in order not to risk the sort of ostentation that he avoided so assiduously throughout his life.

Shaykh Emin has, in his turn, devoted his entire life to emulating this example, and to teaching these inner and outer disciplines to students, issuing *ijāza* to those who successfully complete their study under him – efforts he continued to the time of his death, well over one hundred years old. As this outline of his training as a scholar demonstrates, Shaykh Emin mastered traditional Islamic scholarship across a broad domain of topics encompassing linguistics, logic, rhetoric, law, and spiritual psychology. Central to this is his position within an *isnād*, that is, within an unbroken lineage of transmission of knowledge extending back to the Prophet Muhammad, may God bless him and grant him peace. And, according to the custom of Muslim scholars of this mold, he in turn passed on the knowledge transmitted to him by his mentors, bequeathing a place in this unbroken chain to students in the 21st century. If seldom encountered, it is nevertheless true that such an *isnād* persists to the present day – despite the many great traumas of recent history that conspired and endeavored to break it.

Shaykh Emin had six children and, by his estimate, about 40 grandchildren. A seventh child passed away as a toddler. Shaykh Emin recalls this as a time of trial:

> We must have full and complete belief in God, and knowledge that everything that happens to us comes from Him. Everything, even the greatest pain, comes to us from God. If we face it with patient endurance, we receive the reward in the life to come.
>
> That is why I did not even cry at the death of my son. He died in my arms when he was two years old. Death is not permanent separation, but a temporary departure. We will not be in this world forever. People who do not believe in the next life say that the world is special and unique and independent. But actually this world is not independent of the next world, of the life to come. They are connected.

Having retired from many years of service as *imām* in a mosque in Ankara, he continued to live a life of rigorous worship. He had little free time, using it when it came to read and contemplate the Qur'ān and consult the commentaries of the great scholars on questions that occur to him in his reading.

Shaykh Emin slept very little – by his own estimate, perhaps three hours during the night, and an hour or two before noon if possible[8]. He always slept in a state of ablution, in emulation of the *sunna* of the Prophet, may God bless him and grant him peace, and mindful that, should he die in his sleep, he would want to face his Lord in a state of purity. He rose daily at around 3AM for the night prayer called *tahajjud*, remaining awake in a state of contemplation until the time of the prescribed dawn prayer [*salāt al-fajr*]. He then remained in the place of prayer until the sun had risen, and then a bit longer, finally offering a voluntary cycle of prayer of great merit and immense reward for the worshipper[9].

He passed the rest of his morning in scholarly writing, sometimes receiving visitors. Shaykh Emin wrote only in Arabic, always facing the direction of prayer [*qibla*] in a state of ritual purity. When his work was interrupted for some reason, he performed ablution and two cycles of prayer [*rakaʿtāyn*] before resuming, a demonstration of profound reverence, typical of the foremost representatives of the Islamic scholarly tradition but seldom encountered in the present day, before the grave responsibility of transmitting knowledge. He chose the topics for his writings according to particular benefit [*maslaha*] that he discerned in them for the people of our time.

To the end of his life, his modest home in Ankara witnessed a steady stream of guests, and he never refused any request for learning, regardless of the level of the student. Shaykh Emin and his guests sat on the carpeted floor of a room lined with shelves of books from floor to ceiling. The students and visitors were always served tea and sweets, and even a complete meal at the appropriate times. He taught his students on an invidual basis, through the pace and method of instruction best suited to each person's aptitudes and constraints. This too is an extension of the living tradition of Islamic scholarship, according to which each student is to be approached with due respect for and consideration of differing levels of diligence, intelligence, and comprehension.

Shaykh Emin strictly applied the principle of not uttering trivial words during conversation with his students and other visitors. He ate, spoke and slept very little. Although it was his habit to fast whenever possible, he went out of his way to accommodate those guests who are not fasting in order to set them more fully at ease in his company. This is understood as an application of the ethic of *muwāfaqa*, according to which one is to defer graciously and agreeably to the needs and preferences of friends and companions. Shaykh Emin similarly adhered to the practice of *īthār*, according to which one always gives priority to the needs of one's friends, one's own needs notwithstanding.

In his observance of *muwāfaqa* and *īthār*, Shaykh Emin was a singular exemplar not of the manners of his generation or social class, but of the living *sunna* of all the prophets. The importance of this for people in his company was tremendous, and not to be overlooked. It is possible to learn a great deal about exemplary conduct from books, and even to some extent to imitate what one reads. But not everything we need to know on this matter is written, nor could it be. (Consider a written description of tying a shoelace, swimming, or riding a bicycle, and how little skilled we would become in these tasks based on the written description alone.) It is by keeping the company of those who know it that we acquire the essentials of exemplary conduct in both its written and unwritten aspects. Shaykh Emin did this with Saydā and his other teachers, as each of them did with their own teachers, and each of these lineages extends to the teaching and example of the Prophet Muhammad, may God bless him and grant him peace. All of this gives us a greater sense of what will be lost to us forever if the last chains of transmission of this tradition were ever to be broken.

In thinking ahead to the inevitable time of his own death, Shaykh Emin had this to say:

> I have no desire at all for a luxurious funeral, but only for things to be carried out as indicated in our sacred law. My body is to be washed with warm water, neither very hot nor too cold, and to be prayed over. We offer a special prayer for the deceased in the mosque. After that prayer I want to be buried in a simple grave, and the Qur'an read for me. I want nothing luxurious or elaborate.
>
> In the U.S. I attended two funerals. One of them was for a man from Yemen, and they spent thousands of dollars for a very luxurious funeral. This is not good. The other funeral I

attended was for a Christian. They made huge preparations, and dressed the body and the hair. The deceased wore a beautiful tie and jacket. After all that they burned his body. So I must ask, why do all this, if you are going to burn his body? Why make such elaborate preparations and waste so much money? This is pride on the part of the dead. It is not proper for a dead man to cost a great deal of money. Such behavior is not well regarded in our religion.

When a man dies, he experiences concern for those he has left behind. He desires to see his relatives and friends increase their preparations for the life to come. Before death, we only imagine what the next life will be like, but afterwards, we have a direct experience of its realities. This causes him to consider those still living, and to wish for them to prepare themselves for the next life, to conduct themselves properly, and not to be in difficulty with God.

So I have no special prayers or wishes for this world. Instead, I have prayers and wishes concerning the life to come. So my prayers are like this: *O God, we believe that You have complete and perfect knowledge of all things, and that You have power over all things. All things are as You determine them to be.* And so even things that we consider bad are within His Knowledge and His Power, and therefore may contain benefit for us about which we are unaware. So we simply pray for everything to be for our benefit, whether we think it is good or bad.

We are commanded in our religion to think

ahead to the life to come. One benefit of this is that thinking about the next life clarifies our beliefs about this life. People who lack belief in the reality of the life to come are readily corrupted, failing to overcome selfish ideas and increase in sinful desires. Their earnings come from means not permitted in our religion. They work, they collect material possessions, their selves and their souls are not purified. This is one reason why we are to think constantly of the life to come.

11 *June* 2014 – 13 *Shaʿabān* 1435

PART II
The Spiritual Lineage of Shaykh Muhammad Emin Er

The teachings of the people of *tasawwuf* are authentic only to the degree that they have been passed on through an unbroken lineage of spiritual transmission called a *silsila*, or chain. Shaykh Muhammad Emīn Er al-Mīrānī received his *ijāzat al-ᶜamaliyya* in the Golden Chain of the Naqshibandi *tarīqa* as follows:

from Shaykh Muhammad Saᶜīd Saydā al-Jizrī
who took it

from Shaykh Muhammad Nūrī

from Shaykh Muhyī ad-Dīn

from Shaykh ᶜUmar az-Zankānī

from Shaykh Khālid [al-Baghdādī] [d. Damascus, 1242 AH / 1827 CE]

from Shaykh ᶜAbd Allāh ash-Shāh al-Hindī ad-Dihlawī [d. Delhi, 1241 AH / 1825 CE]

from Shaykh Shams ad-Dīn Habīb Allāh Jān Janān [d. Kafevyan, 1195 AH / 1781 CE]

from Shaykh Muhammad al-Badawānī [d. Lahore, 1135 AH / 1722 CE]

from Shaykh Muhammad Sayf ad-Dīn [d. Sirhind, 1095 AH / 1684 CE] *from* Shaykh Muhammad Maʿsūm [d. Sirhind, 1079 AH / 1668 CE]

from al-Imām ar-Rabānī Shaykh Ahmad al-Farūqī as-Sirhindī [d. Sirhind, 1034 AH / 1624 CE]

from Shaykh Muʾīd ad-Dīn Muhammad al-Bāqī Billāh [d. Delhi, 1014 AH / 1605 CE]

from Shaykh Muhammad al-Khwājakī al-Amkanakī as-Samarqandī [d. Shash, 1008 AH / 1599 CE]

from Shaykh Darwīsh Muhammad [d. Samarqand, 970 AH / 1562 CE]

from Shaykh Muhammad az-Zāhid [d. Samarqand, 936 AH / 1529 CE]

from Shaykh Nāsir ad-Dīn ʿUbayd Allāh al-Ahrār as-Samarqandī ibn Mahmūd ibn Shihāb ad-Dīn [d. nr. Samarqand, 895 AH / 1490 CE]

from Shaykh Yaʿqūb al-Jarkhī al-Hisārī [d. Hulgatu, 851 AH / 1447 CE]

from Shaykh ʿAlāʾ ad-Dīn al-ʿAttār [d. Bukhara, 802 AH / 1400 CE]

from Shāh Naqshband [d. Bukhara, 791 AH / 1388 CE]

from as-Sayyid Amīr Kulāl ibn as-Sayyid Hamza [d. Sukhar, 772 AH / 1370 CE]

from Shaykh Muhammad Bābā as-Samāsī [d. Samas, 755 AH / 1354 CE]

from ʿAlī ar-Ramītanī [d. Khwarazm, 715 (721?) AH / 1315 (1321?) CE] *from* Shaykh Maḥmūd al-Injīr Faghnawī [d. nr. Bukhara, 717 AH / 1317 CE]

from Shaykh ʿārif ar-Rīwakrī [d. Riwakar, 636 AH / 1239 CE]

from Shaykh ʿAbd al-Khāliq al-Ghujdawānī [d. nr. Bukhara, 575 AH / 1179 CE]

from Shaykh Abū Yaʿqūb Yūsuf al-Hamdānī [d. Khurasan, 535 AH / 1140 CE]

from Shaykh Abū ʿAlī al-Fārmadī [d. nr. Tus, 447 AH / 1084 CE]

from Shaykh Abū al-Hasan al-Kharqānī [d. nr. Bistam, 425 AH / 1033 CE]

from Shaykh Abū Yazīd al-Bistāmī [d. Damascus or Bistam, 261 AH / 875 CE]

from Imām Jaʿfar as-Ṣādiq [d. Medina, 148 AH / 765 CE]

from Qāsim ibn Muhammad ibn Abī Bakr as-Ṣiddīq [d. nr. Medina, 108 AH / 726 CE]

from as-Sahābī al-Jalīl Salmān al-Fārisī [d. Jerusalem, 33 AH / 654 CE]

from Sayyidinā Abū Bakr as-Ṣiddīq al-Akbar [d. Medina, 13 AH / 634 CE]

from the Prophet Muhammad, may the praise and peace of God be upon him

from Jibrīl, peace be upon him, who received it from his Lord Mighty and Majestic

PART III

The Soul of Islam: Essential Doctrines and Beliefs

by Muhammad Emin Er

All praise is due only to God, the Lord of the Worlds. And may the peace and blessings of God Most High be with His Messenger, Muhammad, the best of the created, the last of the prophets, and also with his family, companions, and those who will follow their path until the Day of Judgment.

Eternal happiness belongs to steadfast believers, who are fully and profoundly aware of their responsibilities towards God and His creatures. Those who are heedless, oblivious that they are God's servants, only perceive their true situation when it is too late.

We bear animosity towards none but those who oppose justice and transgress the rights of others.

INTRODUCTION

The general and literal meaning of the word *islām* is obedience, without reservation, to something above us.

In its religious sense, the meaning of the word Islam is more specific, calling for:

• complete submission and obedience to God Most High as the One Reality which is above us in every way

• fulfillment without reservation of all of God's commands, first and foremost those which impose a necessary obligation[10]

• offering those religious observances that are recommended[11]

• engaging in the course of action that is best for the believer to undertake, and most esteemed by God, in each moment[12]

• refraining from all that God forbids explicitly

• refraining as well from all that is reprehensible before God, including religious practices for which He has given no authority, actions of dubious worth or permissibility, and even excess in that which is required or commended[13]

This is the Islam that it has pleased God Most High to seek from humankind, and indeed from all of His creation. All creatures, and even inanimate entities, submit themselves fully to God in every moment, according to their natures. Human beings likewise have a primordial nature submissive to God, together with a free will permitting us sometimes to lapse into disobedience and delusion.

Like the branches of a tree, a number of other foundational terms and concepts are properly part of this general concept of Islam, such as the following[14]:

RELIGION: God Most High has given humanity all of His creation as a gift, and promised to receive it back in exchange for the eternal company of the Creator. This is the sense in which "religion" is to be understood: as a compact between the

Creator and His human creatures. We use this much abused word to refer to that system implemented according to the commands of God Most High as the means through which people possessing both discernment and free will are led to contentment and well-being in this world, and to salvation in the Hereafter.

FAITH: This means affirmation by the believer of all that is both essential for us to know, and required for us to observe in personal practice.

SCHOOL: Sometimes also called, in English, a *school of law*, this refers to the particular perspective on religious law and tradition preferred and adopted by qualified scholars.[15]

LAW: We use this word to refer to the message brought by the Prophet Muhammad, may God bless him and grant him peace, to humankind through divine revelation.

WAY: We follow the way through remembrance of God Most High in the recollection and recitation of His Names, and both discerning and engaging in the course of action that is best for the believer to undertake and most esteemed by God for us in each moment.

REALIZATION: This comes about through the growth of a discerning and proper insight, and its continual presence within us. We strive to diminish the barrier of separation between ourselves and that which is beyond the reach of the coarse senses, in the world of the Unseen. As indicated in the statement of one of the Companions of the Prophet Muhammad, may God bless him

THE SOUL OF ISLAM

and grant him peace, "It is as though I see the Throne of my Lord." In other words, we may become capable of approaching that which transcends the physical world, as though perceiving the Unseen.

PURIFICATION OF THE HEART: We cleanse ourselves of all manner of blemish and impurity and adorn ourselves with virtuous habits and righteous deeds.

VIRTUE: This is to worship God and to perform righteous deeds for His Sake as though we see Him.

Among all of these, the state of Virtue is the loftiest and most distinguished. Indeed, each of the terms and concepts just listed exceeds and encompasses the one preceding it in the list. Together these provide a general and hierarchical framework of that which constitutes Islam. None of the concepts just listed falls outside of the scope of that which it has pleased God to impose upon humankind as the path to deliverance from His punishment. These are no more distinct from Islam than the branches of a tree are from its trunk.

It should be well understood that Islam, as chosen by God and designated as the path to His Good Pleasure, is not just a philosophy or a kind of speculative claim.

It is not just the recitation of the testimony of faith[16], that is, to testify that "There is nothing worthy of worship except God, and Muhammad is God's Messenger."

It is not just a belief we hold in the heart, nor simply the performance of particular actions with the limbs.

It is not just knowing God.

It is not (as some pretend in reducing it to an ideology) *just this*, or *just that*....

Islam is submission to God through fulfilling His Commands and refraining from His Prohibitions under all circumstances, public or private. This is possible through faith, righteous deeds, invitation to mutual support and good counsel, and patient perseverance against trial and affliction. God Most High has set this out for us in a chapter of the Qur'ān [17]:

> *[I swear] by what remains of time [that] surely each human being is lost, except for those who believe with faith, and perform righteous deeds, and counsel one another to truth, and counsel one another to steadfast patience.*
> [al-ʿAsr 103:1-3]

This brief chapter offers a clear and concise statement concerning the rights held over us by other people and by God, as well as of the path of perfection in this world and the next. This path is, in fact, the way of salvation in the Hereafter and the betterment of each person through recognizing and working to safeguard these rights. Faith and righteous deeds are the rights of God Most High over us. It is through safeguarding these that we, as servants of God, refine and perfect ourselves. One of the rights that others have over us is to enjoin us to truth and steadfast patience. It is through safeguarding such rights that we invite other people to join us on the path of seeking success in this world and the next. Thus, to respond actively to God's rights over us, and to those of other human beings, allows us to meet the requirements given in the verses above, and to reach success and salvation.

With God's permission, the following pages will address, in greater depth and in order of importance, each of the concepts mentioned thus far – this order being Faith (which is inward), Submission to God (which is outward), and Virtue (which joins the inward and the outward). The first concern of the chapter of the Qur'ān just given is Faith, and this topic is also addressed in a famous narrative brought to us by God's Messenger[18], may God bless him and grant him peace, as follows:

> One day as we were sitting with the Messenger of God, may God bless him and grant him peace, a man approached us in clothes that were extremely white, with hair that was extremely black, who bore no trace that we could see of having traveled, and whom none of us knew.
>
> He sat down so close to the Messenger of God, may God bless him and grant him peace, that he rested his knees upon [the Prophet's] knees, and placed his two hands upon his thighs. [...]
>
> [The stranger] said: "Tell me about Faith."
>
> [The Prophet] said: "It is that you affirm God, His angels, His books, His messengers, and the Last Day, and that you affirm the Decree [al-Qadar], the good and the bad of it."

The second topic is also presented in this narration, and concerns Submission to God [islām]:

[The stranger] said: "Muhammad, tell me about Submission to God."

The Messenger of God, may God bless him and grant him peace, said: "Islam is that you bear witness, testifying that there is no object of worship aside from God, and that Muhammad is the Messenger of God; and you establish the ritual prayer; and you give the alms-tax; and you fast in the month of Ramadan; and you perform the pilgrimage to the House if you are able to find a way to do so."

And the final topic has to do with Virtue [*ihsān*], as well as mutual support and good counsel, and patient perseverance against trial and affliction:

Finally, he said: "Tell me about Virtue."

[The Prophet] said: "It is ... that you worship God as though you see Him, for if you do not see Him, truly He sees You."

The remainder of this brief introduction to our religion will address each of these topics – Faith, Submission to God, and Virtue – in greater detail.

FAITH

The Arabic word *īmān*, translated here as *faith*, has connotations that the English word does not capture. In its most literal sense, the word *īmān* means *approval without condition*. In English it is possible to use the word *faith* intransitively, without an object – one *has* faith, but need not declare the object of that faith. But the word *īmān* is generally considered to be transitive: one has *faith in* something[19].

Used in its religious sense, *īmān* is defined as the whole-hearted embrace, approval, and declaration of the canonical truths brought by Muhammad, God's Messenger, may God bless him and grant him peace. It is therefore a condition of faith that we not neglect or contradict any part of this message. To be oblivious of these truths is to be in a state of denial called *kufr*, a condition that culminates in damnation to the Hellfire for eternity unless we repent, seek forgiveness, and renew our active engagement in faith and awareness of the Divine Presence[20].

As the above narration shows, there are six principles of faith. Each is now described in turn, together with the integrals of each principle.

First Principle of Faith: Belief in God Most High

1. We are to know and to believe with certainty that God Most High is One, and without partners or associates. He[21] has no rivals of any kind who can share in His Power, Authority, or Sovereignty. This is shown in the following verse of the Qur'ān:

> Had there been other deities in them aside from God, [the heavens and the earth] would have both been left in ruin.
> [al-Anbiyā 21:22]

2. We are to know and to believe with certainty that there is no entity like God, that God resembles nothing in His creation, and that He has no need of any kind for the things He has created.

3. We are to know and to believe with certainty that God, as He is, is beyond the ability of human beings to conceive or imagine. Thus, although we encounter such passages as the following in the canonical sources, we accept them with sure conviction but without further inquiry into the way in which they are true:

The All-Merciful reposes upon the Throne.
[Tā Hā 20:5]

*Truly your Lord is He Who created the heavens and
the earth in six ages, and is established upon the Seat of
Authority. [al-Aᶜrāf 7:54]*[22]

4. We are to know and to believe with certainty that
the attribute of *existence* is necessary for God Most
High, and that non-existence is impossible to ascribe
to Him. The proof of this is rendered in the following
verse of the Qur'ān:

*It is God Who has created you and sustained you, and
Who will then cause you to die, and then will give life to
you again. Do any of those which you associate
[with Him as partners] do anything like this? He is
Exalted, Above whatever it is that they wish
[to worship] alongside of Him.*
[ar-Rūm 30:40]

5. We are to know and to believe with certainty that
the attribute of *existing outside of time* is necessary for
God Most High, and that for him to be bounded by
time, which is part of His creation, is impossible to
ascribe to Him. The proof is given in this verse:

He is the First and the Last.
[al-Hadīd 57:3]

6. We are to know and to believe with certainty that
the attribute of *everlasting* is necessary for God Most
High, and that any sense of extinction or annihilation
is impossible to ascribe to Him. The proof is given in
these verses:

He is the First and the Last.
[al-Hadīd 57:3]

All things will perish except for His Presence.
[al-Qasas 28:88]

7. We are to know and to believe with certainty that the attribute of *without resemblance to anything created* is necessary for God Most High, and that resemblance to the creation in any way can never be ascribed to Him. Thus:

There is nothing whatsoever like Him –
and He is the Hearing, the Seeing.
[ash-Shūra 42:11]

8. We are to know and to believe with certainty that the attribute of *self-subsisting* is necessary for God Most High, and that one can in no way ascribe to Him the need for anything, either creating or created:

God is Entirely Independent of all of the worlds.
[āl ʿImrān 3:97 and ʿAnkabūt 29:6]

9. We are to know and to believe with certainty that the attribute of *unicity*²³ is necessary for God Most High, applicable to His Existence and His Actions. One cannot in any way ascribe duality or multiplicity to Him, as shown in the verse:

Your God is One God.
[al-Baqara 2:163; also an-Nahl 16:22
and al-Hajj 22:34]

10. We are to know and to believe with certainty that the attribute of *living* is necessary for God Most High, and that death can in no way be ascribed to Him. A proof of this is seen in the verse:

> *And place your trust in the Living One,*
> *Who does not die.*
> [*al-Furqān* 25:58]

11. We are to know and to believe with certainty that the attribute of *all-knowing* is necessary for God Most High, to Whom no sort of ignorance can ever be ascribed. Thus:

> *And know that God has knowledge of all things.*
> [*al-Baqara* 2:231; *an-Nisā* 4:176]

12. We are to know and to believe with certainty that the attribute of *absolute will* is necessary for God Most High, and that it is impossible to ascribe to Him any sort of limitation to His Will. The proof is given in this verse:

> *And had your Lord so willed it, everyone on*
> *earth would have believed.*
> [*Yūnus* 10:99]

13. We are to know and to believe with certainty that the attribute of *omnipotence* is necessary for God Most High, to Whom it is impossible to ascribe inability or incapacity of any sort.

> *Truly God is Almighty.*
> [*al-Baqara* 2:20, 106]

14. We are to know and to believe with certainty that the attributes of *all-hearing* and *all-seeing* are necessary for God Most High. It is not possible for the matter to be other than the way He described it in addressing Moses and his brother Aaron:

> *He said, "Do not fear! Truly I am with you both*
> *– Hearing and Seeing."*
> [*Tā Hā* 20:46]

And elsewhere:

> There is nothing like Him – and He is the Hearing,
> the Seeing [of all things].
> [ash-Shūrā 42:11]

15.   We are to know and to believe with certainty that the attribute of *speaking* is necessary for God Most High. It is not possible for one to say that He is silent, since:

> God spoke to Moses directly.
> [an-Nisā 4:164]

16.   We are to know and to believe with certainty that whatever comes about – however probable or improbable it may seem to us – is only according to what God wishes and prefers, as the following verses establish:

> Surely God does as He wills.
> [al-Hajj 22:18]

> Surely God ordains whatever He intends.
> [al-Mā'ida 5:1]

In addition to the textual proofs given here for each of the Attributes of God Most High, it is possible to find rational proofs for them in the perfect beauty and order observed in the created universe.

There are benefits that arise through belief in God, His Attributes, and His Divine Names, and these include the following:

• The servant of God is guided through belief to love and respect for God Most High.

• Belief naturally requires that the servant obey the commands and prohibitions ordained by the Most High.

• Obedience to God's commands and prohibitions allows the believing servant to attain to contentment in the life of this world and eternal bliss in the life of the Hereafter.

Second Principle of Faith: Belief in God's Angels

It is obligatory to believe with certainty in the heart, and to proclaim aloud, that:

• The angelic creation exists.

• The angels are sinless and obedient servants of God Most High.

• They worship and praise God continuously.

• They act in complete accord with His Command, never opposing Him or rebelling against Him.

None but God knows their exact number. However, we do know that some of them carry the Throne of God, and some dwell upon the earth. We also know that some of them are charged with recording the deeds of human beings, some with responsibility for rain or vegetation, some with the womb and what it carries, and some with the congregations of remembrance and recitation of the Names and Attributes of God Most High [24].

It is an obligation for believers to know the names of ten angels:

• Rakīb and Atīd, the scribes on our right and left who record our good deeds and transgressions[25]

• Jibrīl, the Angel of Revelation

• Mikā'īl, charged with providing nourishment

for bodies and knowledge for souls

• Isrāfīl, who delivers commands, places spirits within bodies, and from whose trumpet will issue the blast that abolishes form at the end of time

• Izrā'īl, the Angel of Death

• Munkar and Nakīr, who question the departed in the grave

• Ridwān, who is in charge of the Garden of Paradise

• Malik, who is in charge of Hellfire

There are benefits that come about through belief in God's Angels, and these include the following:

• Through this, the believer better understands the Greatness, Power, and Might of the Creator of these beings.

• The servant increases in awareness of God Most High and in gratitude for His Blessings, knowing that among the angels are those delegated to provide for our needs and protect us from harm, as well as to record our actions.

• The servant comes to love God's Angels because they worship God Most High as He deserves, and because they pray and supplicate for the believers.

Third Principle of Faith: Belief in the Revealed Books

It is obligatory to believe with certainty in the heart, and to proclaim aloud, that God Most High has sent down books through His Messengers, by means of which He has explained to us the path leading to our happiness and success. Among these books are the Torah revealed to Moses, the Psalms revealed to David, the Gospel revealed to Jesus, and the final revelation, the Qur'ān, which God Most High sent down to our Prophet Muhammad, may God bless him and grant him peace[26]. Besides these, some books (now lost) were revealed to other Prophets whose names are no longer known. (May peace be upon all of the Prophets of God, be they known to us, or unknown.)

There are benefits that come about through belief in God's revealed books, and these include the following:

- Because these books guide humankind to the right path, we learn that God does not turn away from His creation, but instead sustains all creatures through His Mercy and Compassion.

- We come to understand God's Wisdom in revealing earlier books according to the needs of particular communities in specific places and limited times, and in revealing the Qur'ān as the final and universal message. Indeed, the Qur'ān supercedes these earlier books, addressing the needs of all communities in all places and times until the Day of Judgment. And through this we see the Divine Wisdom which demonstrates the superiority of the Qur'ān to all other books.

- We are surpassingly grateful to God for directing humankind to the right path, allowing us in our time and in our communities to be recipients of the Qur'ān.

Fourth Principal of Faith: Belief in the Prophets

1. To believe in the Prophets means to believe that God Most High has sent Messengers to humankind who brought both glad tidings and admonition.

2. God Most High listed the names of some of His Prophets in the Qur'an, twenty-five in all. They are:

Adam

Noah

Hud

Salih

Abraham

Lot

Jacob

Ishmael

Joseph

Elias

Jonas

Job

Shuayb

Ezekiel

Elijah

Moses

Aaron

David

Solomon

Enoch

Zacharias

John

Jesus

Muhammad

It is an obligation for the believer to know these Prophets by name, and to believe with certainty in those whose names are not given in the Qur'an – peace be upon them all[27].

3. It is obligatory for all Muslims to know the nine characteristics of the Prophets. Of these, four are necessary, four are impossible, and one is possible:

> • It is *necessary* that a Prophet always tell the truth, and impossible for a Prophet to tell a lie. If this were not the case, we would find ourselves in the position of rejecting the miraculous conduct of the Prophets, and of contradicting God Most High in His Command:
>
> > *Believe in God and His Messenger.*
> > [*an-Nisā* 4:136]
>
> > *O people! The Messenger has come to you with the Truth from your Lord, so believe.*
> > [*an-Nisā* 4:170]
>
> • It is *necessary* for a Prophet to be trustworthy, and it is *impossible* for a Prophet to be treacherous and to betray others. If this were not the case, we would have to assert that God Most High has commanded a person to evil, which likewise is not possible.
>
> • It is *necessary* for a Prophet to convey his message to humanity, and it is *impossible* for that message to be withheld, in whole or in part. If this were not the case, we would have to claim that God Most High has commanded false conduct, which He does not do.

• It is *necessary* for a Prophet to be intelligent,
and it is *impossible* for his intellect to be weak.
Otherwise a Prophet would be weak or incapable in mustering definitive proofs against the
arguments of those who oppose him, and this
can never be the case. It is clearly revealed in
the Qur'ān that the Prophets offer devastating
arguments and conclusive proofs against their
enemies.

• It is possible that a Prophet has experienced discomfort and inconvenience on account of human
nature, and it is acceptable for us to believe this.

4. It is obligatory for the believer to know certain
attributes unique to our master, Muhammad, may
God bless him and grant him peace. These include
the following

• He is the beloved of God and the intimate
friend of God[28].

• He is the last of the Prophets, and their Seal.

• He is the most distinguished among God's
creatures.

• He is sent to all of humanity, as well as the
jinn.

• The law he brought abrogates and supercedes
all systems of law that came before it, and is
fully able to address the needs of every people in
all times and places until the Day of Judgment.

• It is required that we know of his miracles.

The scholars[29] attribute to Muhammad, may God
bless him and grant him peace, fully a thousand miracles. These can be grouped into five categories:

1. The Noble Qur'ān is a miracle that addresses the mind. All of humanity, as well as the *jinn*, have proven incapable of bringing forth anything in the least bit comparable to the Qur'ān – nor could they, even if they worked together in perfect collaboration. Among many other examples, it is miraculous that the Qur'ān will endure unchanged and without imitation in its content, composition, and style until the Day of Judgment; that it arouses terror and inspires awe in the hearts of those who hear it; and that it reports so many unseen realities.

2. There are miracles of the Prophet, may God bless him and grant him peace, that address the five senses. Among them we count the flowing of water from between his fingers, the splitting of the moon and holding back the sun, his increasing the abundance of food through his blessedness [*baraka*] and supplication, his healing of the sick, the transformation of objects through his touch, and so forth.

3. The signs of his prophethood witnessed before his birth are among his miracles, may God bless him and grant him peace.

4. The devout among his followers performed miraculous deeds indicating that, through the Prophet, may God bless him and grant him peace, they were on the straight path.

5. The perfect moral disposition bestowed by God Most High upon Muhammad, may God bless him and grant him peace, is among the miracles connected to him. Proof enough can be found in the verse:

> *Truly you are of a sublime character.*
> [*al-Qalam* 68:4]

Fifth Principal of Faith: Belief in Resurrection, Judgment, and the Hereafter

There are twelve essential elements of belief concerning the Hereafter:

1. To believe that God Most High will punish in the grave those He deems worthy to punish.

2. To believe in the two angels who will question us in our grave[30].

3. To believe that all of humanity will rise from the grave and be brought together to be questioned, rewarded, and punished on the Day of Judgment.

4. To believe that there is a complete accounting made of all our actions.

5. To believe in retribution[31] among people in the Hereafter for misdeeds committed in the life of this world.

6. To believe that our actions will be weighed in the Balance.

7. To believe that each person, male and female, will be given the book that records the deeds performed during the life of this world, some in the right hand, some in the left.

8. To believe in the Traverse, sharper than a sword and thinner than a hair, stretched across the gulf of Hellfire.

9. To believe in the existence of the Fountain in Paradise, and of its Pool and the water it contains which, once tasted, allows one never to thirst again.

10. To believe in the intercession of the Prophet, may God bless him and grant him peace, on behalf of his community.

12. To believe that those who have rejected faith, as well as some of the sinful believers of God's choosing, will enter Hellfire.

13. To believe that the sincere believers will enter the Garden.

Among the benefits conveyed to us through our belief in the Hereafter are the following:

• Belief in the Hereafter motivates people to worship God Most High more wholeheartedly and single-mindedly, seeking the great reward of the Day of Arising.

• Belief in the Hereafter helps to prevent us from rising in opposition to God's commands, on account of our fear of punishment on that day.

• Belief in the Hereafter helps the believers escape anxiety concerning their stature, such as lack of worldly wealth and possessions, knowing that the pleasures we have missed in this life are abundantly recompensed through eternal blessings in the life to come.

Sixth Principle of Faith: Belief in Divine Determining

Our belief in the Divine Decree is the certainty that all gain and loss, happiness and sorrow, faith and infidelity, worship and rebellion, benefit and harm, profit and debt – in short, everything that transpires – does so according to God's Will, Divine Wisdom, Determining, Apportioning of provision and Allocation of sustenance to every creature. There is none to reject, rescind, reverse, or refute whatever God Most High has determined and decreed.

The benefits of our belief in the Divine Decree include these:

- It fosters our complete trust in God Most High.

- It comforts us, allowing peace to enter the heart.

- It deters us from arrogance and self-love.

- It prevents us from giving way to complaint and anxiety when our hopes and wishes do not come to pass.

THE FOUNDATIONS OF FAITH ACCORDING TO THE FOLLOWERS OF THE PROPHET'S TRADITION[32]

• God exists, and is One, Alone and Unique, without partner or associate.

• God is beyond our understanding and imagining.

• There is nothing whatsoever comparable to God or His Attributes.

• There is no resemblance between God and any of His creatures, including humankind. He is Ever-Existing, and Aware, without rest or respite or sleep.

• God can create without recourse to means. It is an easy matter for Him to resurrect the dead.

• God was Ever-Existing before He created anything, whether it be living or non-living. He was the Creator before the creation of anything that exists, and this Divine Attribute does not depend upon anything in creation.

• His Attributes are not metaphors used to describe or qualify Him, but instead are real and eternal, without origin or ending. His Attributes fit only Him, and the traits of His creatures fit only themselves. To be ignorant of these Attributes, or to compare the Attributes of God that have been described by God with the traits of His creatures, causes belief in His Might and Power to be lost.

• God does not depend on the knowledge or awareness of any creature, living or non-living, in order to possess any of His Attributes. His Attributes are His without condition.

• Nothing is like Him. He Alone is All-Hearing and All-Seeing.

• He created living beings for service to Him, and they depend upon Him completely. He created them through His Omniscience, allotting to them their provision, destiny, and end.

• Everything happens within His Will and Determining. It is only His Will that is causal, and not that of creatures, who can only serve Him. What His servants desire is brought to effect only if God permits it. What He wills comes to pass, and what He does not will, does not come to pass.

• The Prophet Muhammad, may God bless him and grant him peace, is God's chosen Messenger and servant. He is the last of the prophets and leader of those believers who stand before God in reverential awe, conscious of their duties to Him. He is the foremost of the prophets, their master. He is the one who is beloved of the Lord of all the worlds. All claims of prophethood after his are a sign of deviance and worldly ambition.

• The Qur'ān is the Word of God, revealed by God. It was uttered by God in a manner that is unknown to humankind. The Qur'ān was revealed to God's Messenger, may God bless him and grant him peace, through His inspiration. Believers affirm it in this sense, and accept that it is the truthful Word of God. The Qur'ān is not created in the way that the words of human beings are created. Whoever hears the Qur'ān and claims that it is the words of a man becomes an unbeliever[33].

• Those who dwell in the Garden of Paradise are able to see God, although we do not know the exact manner of their seeing Him.

• The Covenant with God made by His servants in the world of souls is true[34].

• The Night Journey and Ascension of the Prophet[35], may God bless him and grant him peace, is true. He was taken by night and ascended while awake.

• We believe in the Pen and the Tablet[36], and that everything inscribed there will come about according to God's Will. Even if everything in creation collaborated in an effort to prevent from happening something that God has decreed, they would not succeed. Likewise, were they to collaborate in bringing about some occurrence not decreed by God Most High, they would also fail. Everything that is to come about until the Day of Judgment has been written and sealed. It cannot be changed.

• It is obligatory for the believer to know that God Most High had complete knowledge in pre-eternity of what every person will do, and that this was part of His Determining even then. No one can change it and it is not subject to our criticism.

• The Throne and Footstool of God[37] exist. God Most High is Independent of all things, up to and including these.

• We do not dwell on the subject of the Divine Essence or the nature of His Existence. We do not debate the essential foundations of God's religion.

• Whoever prostrates in the same direction as we do in the manner in which we pray[38], accepts whatever the Prophet, may God bless him and grant him peace, has brought, and attests to the truthfulness of whatever the Prophet has said and narrated to us – this person we call *muslim* (one who has submitted) and *mu'min* (one who has belief in Islam).

• The committing of sins by a person who meets the conditions just given never allows us to consider him a non-believer, unless he considers that which is forbidden by Islam to be permissible[39].

• However, we do not say that sins do not harm the faith of the one who commits them. This is because faith requires acceptance of the Oneness of God [*tawhīd*] and of all the other things that the believer is obligated to know and submit to.

• To be certain of our final end, or to lose hope in the Mercy and Compassion of God, are to step outside of Islam. The best path is therefore to remain in a state between fear and hope before God Most High.

• Having once possessed faith, the servant of the Most High is considered to be without it only through its rejection, or through rejection of any of the foundational principles of the religion of Islam that are obligatory for the servant to know and accept.

• All of the commands and principles conveyed to us through authentic and reliable means from the Messenger of God, may God bless him and grant him peace, are true.

• All of the believers who fear God are the friends of God. The most esteemed of them before God are those who are most obedient to Him and who follow the Qur'ān rigorously.

• Those who, in Islam, have committed major sins, do not remain in Hellfire eternally. Their affair is for God to decide. If He desires to, He forgives them through the abundance of His Mercy, or if He desires to, He punishes them according to His Justice.

• So long as they prostrate themselves in the direction of our prostration, we consent to pray behind those who lead us in prayer, and to offer the prescribed prayer for their funerals. This is not contingent on whether one of them is a good person or a sinner.

• We never draw our sword to inflict harm upon one of the followers of the Prophet, may God bless him and grant him peace, except in carrying out punishment or retaliation as prescribed in the sacred law.

• We do not rise in revolt against the leaders of an Islamic government, regardless of their oppressiveness, so long as their oppression does not amount to unbelief. We do not curse them. We do not withhold our obedience from them. So long as they do not order us to transgress and commit sins, we consider obedience to their orders as obligatory for us in Islam.

• We follow the tradition of Islam and embrace the community of believers[40], refraining from deviance, dissension, and novelty.

• We love those people who are just and trustworthy, and despise those who are tyrannical and deceitful.

• The duties of pilgrimage and striving in the path of God are to continue, whether under the administration of a ruler who is corrupt or of one who is just. We cannot simply abandon these duties due to circumstance.

• We believe firmly in the existence of the angels who record our deeds; in the Angel of Death; in the angels who question us in the grave; and in the torments of the grave.

• With regard to the Day of Judgment, we believe firmly in the resurrection; in the full accounting of our deeds; in our final reckoning before God Most High; in His rewards and punishments; in the Bridge across the Hellfire; and in the Balance.

• The Garden and the Hellfire exist already. They have been created, and are everlasting.

God created them as destinations for people before the people themselves were created. God places whomever He wishes in Paradise according to His Mercy, and places whomever He wishes in the Hellfire according to His Justice. The deeds of each of us are committed according to the destination for which each of us was created, and this will be our abode.

• A person's capability to perform an action possesses two aspects[41]. The first aspect is facilitation and direction placed within the action itself by God Most High. The second aspect is the ability, related to the person's aptitudes, to carry out the action and bring this first aspect to completion. A person's accountability for actions issues from this second aspect.

• The actions of God's servants come about through God's creation, and the servant's performance, of the actions. God commands us to perform only that of which we are capable.

• Everything that occurs, occurs within God's Will, Knowledge, Determination, and Decree.

• The prayers and charity of the living can be of help to the dead.

• God accepts supplications from His servants that address their needs. It is impossible for any of His servants to be free of need for Him for even the smallest part of an instant.

• God possesses both Contentment with His servants, and Wrath towards them. His

Contentment and His Wrath are not like those attributed to anything in His creation.

• We love those people who are Companions of the Prophet, may God bless him and grant him peace. We do not love any one of them more than we love the others. We deplore those who have animosity towards the Companions of the Prophet, may God be pleased with them all.

• We accept it as a fact that after the passing of the Prophet Muhammad, may God bless him and grant him peace, leadership of the community [khilāfa] was passed to Abū Bakr as-Siddīq, and then consecutively to ʿUmar, ʿUthmān, and ʿAlī, may God Most High be pleased with them all.

• We bear witness that those ten of his Companions said by the Prophet, may God bless him and grant him peace, to be guaranteed Paradise, shall indeed enter Paradise[42].

• Those who speak well of the Companions and the chaste Wives of the Prophet, may God bless him and grant him peace, banish hypocrisy from the heart.

• We only speak well and never ill of the scholars from among the Righteous Predecessors[43] and the Righteous Successors who came after them.

• We do not consider any of the Friends of God[44] to be superior to any of His Messengers, peace be upon them all. Every Messenger is above the Friends of God. We believe in

the miracles of the Friends of God and the
narratives about them conveyed to us through
trustworthy sources.

• We believe in the signs of the Day of Arising[45],
such as the coming of the False Messiah and the
descent to earth of Jesus son of Mary, peace be
upon him. We believe as well in the rising of
the sun from the west and the emergence of the
Beast, signs of the Day of Judgment.

• We reject belief in fortune-tellers, soothsayers,
and astrologers – in short, in all who claim to
have knowledge of the secrets of the unknown,
and who speculate about past and future events
according to assumptions that conflict with the
normative rulings of Islam.

• We accept as just and correct the congruity
of our belief with what is held through the
consensus of the scholars of our community,
and reject what departs from it as unjust and
superstitious, a reason for Divine Wrath.

• The religion of God is the same in the heavens
and on the earth. God Most High has said:

> *Truly the way of life with God is that of self-surrender.*
> [āl ʿImrān 3:19][46]

And He has said:

> *Today I have perfected your religion for you and
> completed My Favor upon you and chosen
> for you Islam as your religion.*
> [al-Māʾida 5:3; cf. 24:55]

Islam is above both excess and deficiency, steering
a middle course between views that liken God to man

on the one hand, and those that ascribe no Attributes at all to Him, on the other. By the same token, Islam steers a middle course between complete despair and full confidence in our salvation in the Hereafter.

These are the beliefs and tenets of our religion that we express through our words, and attest in our hearts. We are far removed from those who depart from what has been stated and explained here, and we seek refuge from them in God Most High. It is our sincere prayer to God that He may keep us steadfast on His path; that He may end our life on His path; and that He may protect us from following the beliefs and sects of those who stray from His path.

SUBMISSION TO GOD

Just as *faith* means approval of and assent, with knowledge and certainty, to all that was brought from God by the Prophet Muhammad, may God bless him and grant him peace, *submission to God* means that we surrender and accept without reservation all of this within our lives and actions. Thus, *islām* is the second principle of the religion of perfection that saves human beings from Hellfire.

In the narrative given in the Introduction, the Prophet, may God bless him and grant him peace, mentions only five principles of submission to God. It is not to be understood from this, however, that submission to God consists only of these. These are, rather, the five cardinal principles of our *islām*, the fruits and outwards signs of our faith, explained in greater detail in this section of the treatise.

First, submission to God means that we bear witness, with the full and faithful conviction of the heart, that there is nothing whatsoever worthy of worship except God Most High, and that Muhammad, may God bless him and grant him peace, is His Messenger. This is declared with the tongue in the following words:

Lā ilāha illā-Llāh.
Muhammad ar-rasūl Allāh.

In offering this testimony, we establish a bond and a compact between ourselves as servants of the Most High, and God our Lord. And we also declare outwardly what we have embraced inwardly, namely, that we accept whatever has been brought to us from God Most High and taught to us by the Prophet Muhammad, may God bless him and grant him peace.

Second, submission to God means that we offer the prescribed ritual prayer[47] in its time at the hour appointed for each day. We do so by reverentially meeting all of the following conditions for its validity:

• the prerequisites for this worship, such as the state of ritual purity

• its integrals, such as the recitation of the opening chapter of the Qur'an and other integrals

• its traditions, emulating the manner in which it was performed by the Prophet, may God bless him and grant him peace, as conveyed to us through the example of living scholars and texts passed on to us through trustworthy narrators

• its adornments, by which we mean proper courtesy before God Most High, Who sees us and permits us to stand before Him even in our state of grave unworthiness

We also strive to avoid anything that would annul or invalidate our prayer, as prescribed in detail by our scholars.

Third, submission to God means that we give the tithe, when our wealth suffices for it to be incumbent upon us, to people belonging to the eight groups defined by the scholars as eligible to receive it.

Fourth, submission to God means that we fast every day in the month of Ramadan. We do so according to the requirements of the divine law. This includes the valid intention to fast, made by night; attention to conditions of impurity that permit exemption, such as menses or post-natal bleeding; and avoidance of the three main conditions for nullification of the fast, these being food, drink, and sexual activity between the break of day and sunset.

Fifth, submission to God means that we perform the Pilgrimage [*hajj*] according to the requirements of the divine law when we are accountable to do so. This means that we observe its prerequisites, integrals, traditions, and adornments, and refrain from the deeds that would annul or invalidate it. The Pilgrimage also calls for the observance of particular courtesies, such as the following:

- to resolve our debts
- to restore trusts and deposits to their owners
- to seek forgiveness from those we have harmed or offended
- to prepare the last will and testament
- to pray the shortened prayer of the traveler
- to take righteous and pious people as our traveling companions

• to set off with abundant lawful food for the journey

• to refrain during the rites from forbidden acts, which include sexual intercourse, aggression, and quarrelling

• to share and spend what we have, avoiding both stinginess and excess

• to pray and supplicate God Most High continually, through remembrance [*dhikr*], recitation of His Book, and turning to Him in repentance

• to perform the ritual prayer as much as possible in congregation

• to guard the tongue from gossip and backbiting, and not to preoccupy ourselves with useless things

VIRTUE

The third cardinal principle of the complete religion of Islam is *ihsān*, meaning excellence or virtuous character. As we have seen, the Prophet, may God bless him and grant him peace, defined this term for us as follows:

> *"It is ... that you worship God as though you see Him, for if you do not see Him, truly He sees You."*

In other words, Virtue is to worship God Alone with true sincerity, keeping nothing but Him in the heart, and responding to His Presence as though we are able to see Him. Failing this, we are to remain constantly assured and aware that He sees us wherever we are, present through His Knowledge and other attributes.

We are responsible for cultivating this state of consciousness of God's Vigilant Awareness of us in every moment, knowing that God sees both the evil that we expose outwardly through our transgressions, and harbor hidden from view within our hearts. This causes us to feel shame and to restrain ourselves, pulling ourselves back from sinful conduct, much as we would in the presence of some person who has authority over us.

When we fail to realize that God observes us, we typically cannot prevent ourselves from wrongdoing. This reflects our ignorance of the real state of affairs in this life, something we should strive to overcome.

Of course, it is also possible that we have some awareness that God Most High sees what we do, but sin anyway. This shows that our knowledge of God is incomplete or inappropriate, and calls for two responses.

First, we are to seek the knowledge that is held to be obligatory for believers, with awareness of the relative importance assigned to some areas of inquiry over others. For instance, we should try to gain understanding of the Divine Attributes as a matter of high priority, and leave aside the more intricate and tenuous argumentation typical of speculative theology[48]. Our goal is to know our obligations before God and the means of satisfying them, and never to fail in fulfilling these obligations while abstaining from the forbidden.

Second, we are to keep the company of righteous people, pondering with them the verses of the Qur'ān and what they indicate. Just as knowledge of religious obligations keeps us from the forbidden, the company of these people inclines us towards what is most right and virtuous in deeds.

As servants of God, we are to come to know our Lord through His Attributes, which (in a manner befitting Him) are perfect and sublime. If we approach this in the manner already explained, we reach, with the permission of God Most High, the state of Virtue described by the Prophet, may God bless him and grant him peace. This state diverts us from all transgression and directs us towards all that is good and auspicious. It is known, for instance, that this lofty awareness of the Divine Presence is precisely what protected Yūsuf from acting upon his base intentions towards Zulaykha[49].

To know God protects the heart from danger. The spiritual heart is the locus of our interaction with God. As we become aware of our responsibility to purify the heart and banish from it the corruption which we would like God never to observe within us, we strive to purify it. This means that we strip away from the heart every ugly trait and work to beautify and adorn it with every praiseworthy quality. Eventually our heart is made clean, polished like a mirror reflecting God to us.

Imam Nawawi[50] said this with regard to the cultivation of *iḥsān*:

> *Virtue means worshipping God in the manner of those who reached the state of seeing God and remaining aware that God is with them. Virtue, modesty, and sincerity require meeting the conditions for protecting the heart and organs[51], and following all of the established rites and courtesies of worship. The followers of the righteous path encouraged socializing with*

virtuous people in order to incur loss of interest in wrongdoing through a sense of shame in their presence. If the state of those who are with human beings becomes like this, one can well imagine the state of those whose hearts are always with God Most High, Who knows all things, exposed or concealed.

So Virtue, as the state of keeping God always in our consideration and acting only for His Sake, is understood to be the fruit of knowledge and the goal of our perseverance. There are two foundational principles to be observed in our seeking of Virtue, these being to turn to God Most High in repentance, and to turn away from the attachment of the heart to creation. Without these, Virtue cannot be attained. In more detail, we are to understand these principles as follows:

First Principle: Repentance to God Most High

We are to regret and repent of all sins, seeking the approval of God Most High and fearing the divine wrath. We are also to be steadfast in our determination not to commit the same sins again, and to restore their rights to people, and to God.

The rights of God Most High over His servants are the obligations of our submission to Him, such as the daily ritual prayers, the tithe, fasting in the month of Ramadan, pilgrimage to the House in Mecca, and so forth. These also include atonement for various transgressions clearly defined in the sacred law, such as breaking the fast, accidental manslaughter, slander, and unlawful oaths and divorce.

The rights of other people over us concern material things we have obtained from them improperly, and verbal abuse such as gossiping, backbiting, tale-bearing, and so forth. In the case of goods unlawfully obtained, we are to restore the rights of their proper owners by returning the goods to them, or (if they have passed away) to their heirs, or if the heirs cannot be found, then to the needy in the form of alms. In the case of verbally abusive behavior, we are to seek the forgiveness of those we have harmed, and to strive to do good things for them.

The sign that our repentance has been accepted is that God Most High protects the organs He has bestowed on us, blessing us and diverting us from forbidden actions as well as those that are frivolous. In this way our repentance becomes genuine [52], as our determination not to repeat open or hidden sins is made secure.

We are to be aware that the sins of which we repent can be grouped into five categories, depending upon the nature of the repentance that each requires.

1. The first concerns the rights of God, such as the prohibition on consuming intoxicants or indulging in musical entertainments. For these, sincere repentance alone is required.

2. The second category consists of sins for which repentance to God, and seeking the pardon of those people who have been harmed, are both required. These include:

- breaking promises
- harming another person without lawful reason
- abusing or expropriating deposits or trusts
- backbiting and talebearing[53]

- disobedience and defiance
- oppression and tyranny by leaders and administrators
- withholding testimony

3. Third, there are sins that require repentance, seeking pardon from those harmed, and return of goods to rightful owners. These include:

- charging interest on loans
- deceit in weights and measures
- consuming the wealth of an orphan
- betrayal of others in a partnership
- the obstruction by husbands of the rights of wives, such as through dowries
- theft
- bribery
- gambling

4. Fourth, there are sins that require recompense to God beyond repentance by offering the missed or invalid action in a valid manner. For instance, sexual intercourse during Pilgrimage before the standing on the plains of ʿArafat not only annuls the Pilgrimage, but requires that it be repeated. This is also required for actions such as missed prayers, which must be made up at the soonest opportunity; omitted days of fasting; the annual tithe to purify our wealth; and so forth.

5. The fifth category consists of sins that require repentance, valid completion, and additional atonement. These are:

• *Swearing a false oath*: This requires that, following repentance, we feed ten needy people in the amount of their required daily subsistence.

• *Withholding conjugal rights*: In particular, this refers to the husband's having taken an oath not to engage in intercourse with his wife for four months, or longer. We atone for this as though it were a false oath, which is to say by feeding ten needy people for a day. The husband who cannot afford this is instead to fast for three days.

• *Unlawful divorce*: This is defined as the husband's repudiation of his wife by uttering a phrase of insult known among the pre-Islamic Arabs[54]. Atonement for this is made by freeing a slave, fasting for sixty days, or feeding sixty needy people for a day.

• *Breaking the fast of Ramadan*: One who eats, drinks, or engages in intercourse during the hours of daylight when fasting is required atones for it through the same manner as that prescribed for unlawful divorce.

• *Accidental manslaughter*: This is to kill a person accidentally and without intention. (There are those who say that homicide is also included in this.) The atonement for this is to free a slave, or to fast for two months consecutively. The option of feeding the needy does not exist in this case.

• *Transgressions of the state of Pilgrimage*[55]: A number of actions are forbidden the pilgrim, which can be categorized according to the atonement they require.

Second Principle: Detaching the Heart from Creation

We are instructed and called to the following in the cultivation of Virtue, once we have offered our repentance as stipulated above.

We are to leave aside whatever earthly blessings and benefits distract us from God Most High. As He has said:

> Say: "Shall I tell you of better things than those [earthly
> joys]? For those who guard themselves [for God],
> with their Lord are gardens through which rivers
> flow, in which they abide forever with pure mates and
> contentment from God. And God sees His worshippers."
> [āl ʿImrān 3:15]

We are to avoid, except in cases of absolute necessity, the company of bad friends, people of malice, and those who are heedless of God[56].

We are to restrain our lower self [nafs] from vanity and ambition, imposing upon it the esteem and love for God that will keep it in check, and conducting our affairs always in the state between fear of God's Wrath and hope for His Mercy.

We are to keep ourselves far from Satan, learning his deceitful tricks in order to turn away from him and towards God. Whenever we are uncertain of how this is to be done, our first recourse is to turn to the commands and prohibitions of the sacred law. After this we are to consult people of knowledge and experience in these matters, then to consider the actions and attitudes of the righteous followers of the Prophet, may God bless him and grant him peace, and finally to consult our conscience.

Our means of seeking livelihood, provision,

and wellbeing in this world are to be lawful, and undertaken with the knowledge that we are not to trust in means, but only in God Most High.

We are to entrust all our affairs to God Most High, and to supplicate Him sincerely and clearly for benefit to us in every outcome.

We are to practice patient forbearance in the face of trials and torments that will come to us in the path of servitude to God. We are to endure resolutely in abstaining from sins.

We are to submit to whatever God has determined for us through His Determining and Decree, praising God and admitting to Him that while we may not know what knowledge and wisdom there are behind them, we hope and believe that there will be blessings in them for us.

We seek only God's contentment with us, and not praise or high esteem among people.

When we do good deeds, we attribute it not to ourselves but to God. We seek forgiveness for our mistakes and praise God and profess to Him our awareness that it is only through Him that anything good has come about. When we lapse into sin, we attribute it not to God but to ourselves. We ask to be forgiven for the transgression, into which we entered of our own free will, albeit within the Knowledge and Determining of Almighty God.

We are to desire and to love for our fellow servants of God that which we desire and love for ourselves. We do not wish for a long life, reflecting on death and the life to come. We strenuously avoid every misguided trait of character, every bad habit, and every novelty in the way of religion. We are to follow the safest and most secure path in dealing with issues that are controversial. And we are to remember God in all of our states.

And success is only from God.

PART IV

For the Revival of Hearts

All praise is God's, Lord of the Worlds, and may blessings and peace be with the Prophets and Messengers, from the descendants of Adam until their seal in Muhammad, the Unlettered Prophet sent with guidance and true religion as a Mercy to the Worlds; and may God's pleasure and peace be upon all of his Family and Companions.

To begin:

Know, O Seeker of the most direct and lofty path to God, that its authentic source is the way of the greatest of the Righteous Predecessors, those who were distinguished by hearts that abstained from the things of this world and by godwariness[57].

Those who are on this path safeguard the integrity of their prescribed prayer, standing in awe of the Divine Presence. They turn away from useless talk. They honor trusts placed in them and keep their promises. They give in charity from God's provision for them, and they believe with certainty in the Hereafter. They strive with their person and their wealth in the affairs of God, and they rely completely upon their Lord Alone. They show patience in the face of trial and affliction, and they find contentment in the unfolding of their decree. They enjoin the right and forbid the wrong, and they do not fear the curses of those who deplore them. They fear only the punishment of their Lord, and when called to bear witness to the Truth, they stand forth, ready. They suppress their anger and forgive people, and they respond with goodness to those who wrong them.

Theirs is the guidance for you to follow.

Because following them means obeying and following the Messenger of God Most High, may God bless him and grant him peace, it is a means to the love of God and manifests His command:

> *Say: If you love God, follow me; then God will love*
> *you and forgive you your sins.*
> [āl ʿImrān 3:31]

BRIEF OVERVIEW OF THIS PATH

The path of which we speak here is continuous worship of the Most High outwardly and inwardly through complete commitment to the exemplary conduct [*sunna*] of the Prophet, may God bless him and grant him peace, and the pursuit of rigorous observance of the sacred law. This means:

- We are to fulfill the required observances, whatever is possible of the recommended ones, and all that is best and most precautionary[58], and the action that is most correct according to the *sunna* in its moment.

- We are to abandon whatever is forbidden, disapproved, doubtful, or (concerning the permissible) in excess of our needs.

◆ We are to avoid completely that novelty or dispensation which contravenes the revealed *sunna* of the Prophet, may God bless him and grant him peace, and rigorous observance.

◆ We are to invoke God Mighty and Majestic continuously, in all circumstances and in all activity and inactivity. We are then to invite others to God Most High with gentleness and patience in the face of resistance, having first adorned ourselves with the attributes of those qualified to do so. Not everyone is capable or qualified to do this, as will be explained below if God Most High so wills.

Then *know*, O Seeker, that we will never be able to travel this path in such a way as to be among those who are both perfected, and able to bring others to perfection, except by traversing five sequential thresholds.

The First Threshold: Certain Faith

Certainty in faith concerns that which is known axiomatically, or through definitive textual proof[59], or by means of a reliable narration [*hadīth*] having only one narrator but well accepted by the community.

> There are seventeen of these certain principles,
> of which five relate to the two testimonies of faith.

We are to believe with certainty that there is nothing worthy of worship, and no creator of things, and none characterized by perfection, and none beyond imperfection, other than God Glorified and Most High.

We are to believe with certainty that the Most High has power over all things, either through intermediate causes or without them (as He wishes). And aside from the Most High, none has power to do anything, with or without the aid of intermediate causes, except by His desire. This is, for instance, demonstrated through His ability to heal a sick person *without* medicine, as compared to the inability of others to heal the sick *with* medicine in the absence of His Will that the cure be effected.

We are to believe with certainty that Muhammad, the Unlettered Prophet, is the Messenger of God, and the Seal of the Prophets, may God bless him and grant him peace. He is the best of all creation, sent with guidance and the true religion to all of creation, a Mercy to the Worlds.

We are to believe with certainty that his law supersedes the laws that preceded it; that it suffices for all subsequent times and places; and that it will endure until just before the Hour.

We are to believe with certainty that all success, salvation, and felicity in this world and the next are through following and obeying the Messenger of God, may God bless him and grant him peace, and that all loss and regret and ruin is in disobeying him.

And six of these certain principles relate to the pillars of faith.

We are to believe with certainty that the Most High is necessarily existent, and that He is Pre-Eternal together with

- His Names and Attributes, such as Life and Majesty, and His Self-Subsistence
- His actions, such as giving blessings and life,

and causing to die

+ other attributes of His that occur as pairs of opposites, such as giving happiness and causing distress

We are to believe with certainty that His angels exist; that they are protected from disobedience to God Most High; that their obedience to the Most High is constant and entirely without fatigue; and that they seek forgiveness on behalf of believers on earth.

We are to believe with certainty in the books that He has revealed to His Messengers, including the Torah, the Gospel, the Psalms, the Qur'ān, and others.

We are to believe with certainty in His Messengers, starting with our father Adam up to our Prophet Muhammad, may God's praise and peace be upon him and upon them all. You are to believe in their honesty, their trustworthiness, their intelligence, their conveying in full of what was commanded of them, and their protection from all sins.

We are to believe with certainty in:

+ the Last Day
+ the questioning by the two angels in the grave
+ the torments or bliss in the grave
+ the resurrection of bodies
+ the Intercession[60]
+ the Pool[61]
+ the reading of each person's book of deeds
+ the Balance and the reckoning
+ retribution and the Traverse across the pit of Fire to Paradise

- the Garden and what is found in it, such as the maidens and servants, the vision of God Most High, and other blessings

- the Fire and what is in it of punishment and torments and other manifestations of Wrath

We are to believe with certainty in the Decree, both the good and the evil of it. Both its good and its evil are from God Most High, with His Knowledge and by His Will. However, the good of it is by His Command and with His Pleasure, while the evil is not by His Command, and is without His Pleasure.

We are to believe with certainty in His Writing in the Preserved Tablet: *Act, for the design of each thing facilitates its purpose.* Good deeds are a sign of certainty of faith and felicity, while the absence of good deeds is a sign of the opposite of these.

And five of these certain principles relate to legal rulings regarding what is obligatory, commendable, forbidden, disliked, and permissible.

We are to believe with certainty in the obligatory nature of all actions whose requirement is absolute, such as uttering the two testimonies of faith, performing the ritual prayers, paying the alms tax, fasting in the month of Ramadan, and Pilgrimage to the House.

We are to believe with certainty in the commendable nature of all actions whose performance is not strictly required[62], such as the supererogatory prayers at the times of the prescribed ritual prayers, the forenoon prayer, the prayer between sunset and nighttime, the night vigil, and so forth.

We are to believe with certainty that any action that it

is absolutely necessary to abandon is also prohibited. These include matters such as ostentation, jealousy, exposing what must be left covered of the body, and the like.

We are to believe with certainty in the offensiveness of all actions whose abandonment is not absolutely required, such as greeting by bowing in deference rather than wishing peace, or offering ritual prayer at the precise moments of sunrise and sunset.

We are to believe with certainty in the permissibility of all actions to which a choice of performance or omission pertains, such as marrying a distant cousin, hunting after leaving the state of purity assumed by the pilgrim in the Hijāz, buying and selling after offering the Friday congregational prayer, and the like.

The Second Threshold: Removing Impediments in the Path

The impediments in the path of Allāh Most High are:

- *sins*, which are removed by repentance
- *love of this world*, which is removed by renouncing it
- *love of company*, which is removed by seclusion
- *Satan*, who is overcome by disobeying him
- *the lower self*, against which you are to strive[63]

Removing these impediments requires all of the following:

We are to repent from all our sins, seeking the contentment of the Most High, fearing His punishments, and regretting all our offenses. We are to determine never to return to the like of them, making up those obligatory observances we have omitted, and making amends to the best of our ability to those with whom we have quarreled or with whom we have been at odds. And faced with any matters that we are unable to set right, we passionately implore God Most High to make amends on our behalf with those we have offended, through His abundant favors on the Day of Arising.

We are to detach the heart from all that distracts us from the Truth[64], such as the things of this worldly life and so forth. We are to ponder the condition of those who are less fortunate than us in terms of their provision in this world, and we are to be grateful. We are to look towards those who are above us with regard to the Hereafter, and blame the *nafs* for its inclination to worldly pleasures, remembering the saying of the Most High:

> Say: "Shall I tell you of better things than those [earthly joys]?" For those who are godwary, with their Lord are gardens through which rivers flow, and in which they abide forever with their pure spouses and Allāh's good pleasure. And Allāh sees His servants well.
> [āl ʿImrān 3:15]

We are to avoid, except through necessity, the company of heedless folk [ahl al-ghafla].

We are to disobey Satan by turning away from his whisperings by seeking refuge with God Most High from his evils; and by knowing the tricks through which he calls to us.

The first of these is his beckoning us to fatalism, and he will say: *If you are created for Paradise, then sin will not harm you; and if not, then obedience will not benefit you.*

When this fails, he will next incite us to rely on

a sense of false confidence in the generosity of God, saying: *The Most High is Generous and Merciful.*

He will summon us to give way to despair, and then to procrastination, saying: *You have plenty of time – do that later.*

Then he will incite us to haste, saying: *Hurry up, you have other concerns!*

Next is the call to ostentation, and he will say: *Do this, so that such and such can be said of you.*

Then to arrogant self-satisfaction, and he will say: *You are the one who did such and such a thing.*

Satan will beckon us as well to other acts of disobedience, both of the limbs and of the heart. It may even be that the Accursed One will approach us by way of a good and virtuous action, as a way to divert one of us from something superior to it. May God protect us from his wickedness through His grace!

We are to struggle against the *nafs*, first by subduing it through eating little; then by imploring God Most High to assist us against it; and then to restrain it with the reins of godwariness against our encroachment upon or indulgence in the forbidden, and precaution concerning the permissible and beneficial. This will impede the *nafs* from its whims and from all things having harmful consequences. And because excess of the permissible may also be harmful, we are to turn away from it in fear while it is still of a degree that poses us no harm.

In this way we are to purify our bodies from whatever does not help us – let alone from what is forbidden to us – followed by our limbs, then our heart, then the heart of the heart[65]. *This is the path of traveling from the signs to their Source*[66].

The alternative is for us to begin by liberating the heart of the heart from all that is other than Him through constant remembrance of the Most High. In this we are present with Him, thereby freeing our heart, then our limbs, and then our bodies from whatever does not help us. *This is the path from the Source to the signs.*

From both of these paths issue people of realization whose way we follow until the contentment of God and His Great Blessing are won. And success comes from Him Alone.

Purifying the body means to purge it of spiritual filth, physical filth, and those physical features that religious law deems superfluous[67]. This enables us to reach the desired state of cleanliness.

Purifying the limbs means to free them from involvement in all disobedience and doubtful matters, thus achieving the state of complete obedience to God Most High.

Purifying the heart means to liberate it from vileness and turbidity, thereby bringing it to a state of clarity.

Purifying the heart of the heart means to guard it against all types of heedlessness of God Most High, thus achieving wakefulness and constant presence before the Glorified and Most High.

Know that the *nafs* is our mount and is ours to ride. We are not to neglect and overlook it – indeed, in order to adhere to either of these two paths, we are obliged to give the *nafs* its rights, while keeping it from its pleasures. Its rights are found between its necessity and its satiety, while its pleasures are found in excessive indulgence in the permissible. And the verified consensus of those who have successfully purified the *nafs* is to adhere to these five principles:

- eating little
- speaking little
- sleeping little
- mixing little with people
- eating only what is permissible, pure, free from even the suspicion of prohibition

The Third Threshold: Preventing Missteps

At this threshold, we work to remove four types of missteps. The first is due to our preoccupation with seeking our provision, and this is removed by means of trust. Next, we err because we desire something of uncertain outcome, and we remove this by deferring our affair completely to God. Third, we worry about the onset of afflictions, and we overcome this through patient perseverance. The last is that we experience resentment in the face of destiny, and we remove this by striving for contentment with what the Most High has determined for us.

We are to rely exclusively upon God Most High with regard to our provision, and in all other matters; and we are to trust in Him to such a degree as to remove all regrets and worries that distract us from the Truth, especially after undertaking everything according to lawful means.

We are to defer in all matters to God Most High to such a degree that we remove all obsessions and regrets concerning affairs whose consequences might be good for us, or might not be.

We are to persevere in adorning ourselves with a

beautiful state of patience, to such a degree that we remove all complaints occasioned by affliction and trials.

We are to show contentment instead of anger in the face of painful events, expressing gratitude to the Most High for their not having been of still greater magnitude.

The Fourth Threshold: Preventing the Corruption of Deeds

We may reach the threshold of the corruption of our deeds in five ways, each having its appropriate remedy:

- *ostentation*, which is removed by purity of intention

- *pride*, which is removed by the remembrance of God's bounties

- *arrogance*, which is removed by calling to mind our powerlessness and essential indigence[68]

- *envy*, which is removed by showing compassion towards the creation of God

- *long hopes*, which are removed by recollecting our death in every moment, *every instant*

We are to desire the pleasure of God Most High both in what we undertake actively, and in that from which we abstain. And we are to free both types of striving from ostentation and concern for reputation, knowing that they may result in annulment of the reward of our good actions, and like consequences.

We are to be grateful to the Most High in those moments when our *nafs* is impressed by what we believe ourselves to have done. Remember the grace of God Most High in freely bestowing His favor upon us, for whatever good has come through us is yet another among our many favors from the Most High.

We are to see ourselves as lower than the rest of the creation of God, not higher, thus bringing to mind the prospect of a bad end[69] for us in death – one, that is, without faith – and considering the sins within us before giving thought to what we may know of the sins of others.

We are to be compassionate with the servants of God Most High, and we are to love for them what we love for ourselves, while recalling the harms of envy and that the true life is the life of the Hereafter. This is because, without any doubt, all the delights of the present world are fleeting. And do not think ill of another in the absence of definite proof according to legal norms – meaning that there must be personal observation, or multiple witnesses, or else reports conveyed to you through a succession of trustworthy persons. We are to give good advice to others, calling them to good, enjoining upon them what is right while forbidding them whatever is wrong, and all of this with gentleness and patience in the face of harm.

We are to shorten our hopes and curtail our desire to amass the things of this world, always remembering its evil and its evanescence, and calling to mind His saying:

> *Woe to every backbiting slanderer, who has gathered wealth and counts it – thinking that his wealth has made him immortal. Not at all! He shall be cast into the Fire.*
> [al-Humaza 104:1-4]

Remember also the saying of the poet Labīd: "Truly apart from Allāh all is in vain."

And we are to contemplate death and what follows it from among the afflictions of the Day of Arising, such as the extreme heat of the Fire of Jahannam and the like.

The Fifth Threshold: The Attributes of Those Who Summon to God

It is not given to every servant to summon others to God. We are to be highly learned in that truth to which we summon, and we are to practice it scrupulously, thereby counting ourselves among the summoned. And we are to respond to adverse and defiant reactions with the best of what is possible for us.

We are to be fully reliant upon God Most High, and to have hope that our summoning to the Truth will bear fruit.

We are to preserve equanimity, renouncing all concern with what is in the hands of others, remaining contented and pleased with basic means. What we are to desire instead is always to seek the highest degree in spiritual matters, and nothing lower.

We are to be gentle, courageous, humble without seeming debased; and we are not to withhold the teaching of that which we know well.

According to our station, we are to be ever conscious of the Divine Presence in summoning to the Truth, putting aside ostentation, pride, and arrogance; upholding dignity; and refraining from superfluous talk.

We are to turn away from pointless chatter, honoring all commitments and promises.

We are to enjoin the right and forbid the wrong,

with gentleness and wisdom, through good counsel and established proofs directed at those whom we have hopes of convincing.

We are to be of the highest character, as manifested by:

- controlling anger, forgiving other people, and showing generosity towards them

- restoring ties with those who have broken with us, and giving to those who withhold from us, and forgiving those who wrong us

- speaking truthfully, safeguarding trusts with which we have been entrusted, honoring our commitments, and keeping our promises

- overlooking the harm done to us by ignorant people when we call them to do something or forbid them from it – and this is one of the greatest virtues

- showing humility when we summon the people to what we know and what we practice, and responding to their wickedness with the best of manners

We are to know that the objectives of summoning others to the Truth are:

- rectifying the people's understanding of the tenets of faith in accordance with the consensus of our scholars and our tradition[70] without indulging in the minutiae of the science of theology – restricting ourselves instead to what has been most rigorously authenticated of the prophetic example
- establishing correct action

+ beautifying the soul

+ establishing unity and brotherhood among Muslims

+ opposing atheism

+ ridding the religion of dubious things which people have contrived about it

We are to know that the most effective means of summoning to the Truth are:

+ to spread those capable of reforming others among the people, particularly in remote villages and desolate regions

+ to disseminate treatises consisting of the basics of religion and the applications of the divine law and the spiritual dimensions of the divine law

+ to create relevant publications and to distribute them

We are furthermore to offer pious discourses and bring awareness to the people concerning their Righteous Predecessors, the Prophet, may God bless him and grant him peace, and his Companions, above all the following instances[71] and similar examples:

+ their endurance under persecution in the course of summoning others, such as the hardships visited upon the Prophet (may Allāh bless him and grant him peace) while summoning the people of Tā'if

+ the endurance of Bilāl and ʿAmmār and others like them from those who emigrated from persecution in Mecca in the path of seeking to affirm the Oneness of the Most High

- their endurance of hardship and hunger during the digging of the Trench around Medina
- the endurance of thirst by Khālid ibn al-Walīd and those with him when they returned from Iraq to Syria, bringing assistance to the fighters there
- their endurance of suffering due to the lack of mounts, food and water and the like, in their passage to Tabūk to engage the Byzantines

SUMMARY OF THIS DISCOURSE

It is necessary that God be our objective, and the Messenger our example, and the Qur'an our charter, and summoning our method, and dying in the path of God our loftiest aspiration.

So this is our path, O Seeker, and we cling to it with tooth and nail, to the fullest extent of our power and ability; and we summon to it every intelligent person, whether Muslim or not.

Those who turn away from it have turned away from the Truth. And whoever answers our summons, he is our brother in God, embraced with intense love, honored and esteemed like our own parents, and treated like our own children in our compassion and mercy towards him.

But whoever turns away and rejects our summons, he is still our brother in religion or in substance – but not in God. We turn with sincere prayers to God, and we ask guidance for ourselves and for you and for all.

And we end our summons affirming that all praise belongs to God, Lord of the Worlds.

S o

this is our path,

O Seeker, and we cling to it

with tooth and nail, to the fullest

extent of our power and ability; and we

summon to it every intelligent person, whether

Muslim or not. Those who turn away from it

have turned away from the Truth. And whoever

answers our summons, he is our brother in God,

embraced with intense love, honored and esteemed like

our own parents, and treated like our own children in

our compassion and mercy towards him. But whoever

turns away and rejects our summons, he is still our

brother in religion or in substance – but not in God.

We turn with sincere prayers to God, and we ask

guidance for ourselves and for you and for

all. And we end our summons affirming

that all praise belongs to God,

Lord of the Worlds.

Notes to the Text

ENDNOTES

1 Shaykh Emin's present last name, Er, is a Turkish version of an ancient family name, whose meaning implies one who embodies *chivalry*. In classical Turkish Sufi literature – for instance, the poems of Yunus Emre – the term *er* is used metaphorically to indicate a saint. In modern Turkish, the word *er* means *soldier*. The Arabic word *fatā* (related to *futuwwa*, and familiar to some English readers through the Sufi manual of Sulāmī) has effectively the same meaning. This name was chosen for Shaykh Emin's family by a relative when, early in the Republican era, a law was imposed governing surnames for Turkish citizens.

2 That is, of what is known to the scholars as *tasawwuf*, or the Islamic tradition in spiritual psychology.

3 Molla Shaykh Muhammad Ma'shuk was the son of the famous Shaykh Ma'sum Nurshini of the village of Nurşin in the region of Bitlis, in southeastern Anatolia. He was also a grandson of the well-known Sufi master Shaykh Abdurrahman at-Taghī. In addition to being a great scholar in his own right, Molla Shaykh Muhammad Ma'shuk was also a successor to the Sufi Shaykh Ahmad Khaznawi. He died in Mekka and is buried in Jannah al-Mu'allah.

4 Al-Ghazālī, *Deliverance from Error* (trans. R. J. McCarthy), Fons Vitae n.d. (reprint of 1980 edition).

5 Mutual consultation is a core principle of fellowship for the sake of God. This theme, so important to Saydā's teachings in the path of *tasawwuf*, is developed at great length in the accompanying treatises. Mutual consultation is an inadequate translation of the Arabic word *nasīha*, which occurs not only in the Qur'ān [see *Yūsuf*, 12: 11], but in a *hadīth* where it is equated to religion [*dīn*] itself.

6 Concerning this concept, see §XIX of the accompanying treatise *Laws of the Heart*, called "The Subtle Faculties of the Soul".

7 As the "Fifth Threshold" in this treatise *For the Revival of Hearts* makes clear, not all seekers are qualified to call others to the Truth, let alone to instruct others in ways that affect the heart.

8 The late morning nap is a *sunna*, called *qaylūla*.

9 This prayer is called *salāt ad-duḥā*, and it is sadly neglected in the present day. It is considered to have the status of *sunna mu'akkada*, that is, a frequent practice of the Prophet (may God's praise and peace be upon him) whose merit is highly emphasized. According to the collections of *ḥadīth*, one who prays *salāt al-fajr* in congregation and then waits until the sun has risen, offering *salāt ad-duḥā*, receives the reward of both *ḥajj* and *'umra*. Another *ḥadīth* informs us that one who sits in the place where he offered *salāt al-fajr* in congregation, remembering God, and then rises in that place to offer *salāt ad-duḥā*, is made forbidden to the Fire.

Prayer at the beginning of the day is prescribed not only for Muslims, but for all of humanity. The proof of this is given in a *ḥadīth qudsī* addressed not to the community of any particular prophet, but to all of humankind. The Prophet Muhammad (may God's praise and peace be upon him) said: "Your Lord said, 'O children of Adam, pray for me four cycles of prostration [*raka'āt*] at the beginning of the day and I shall care for your needs for the rest of that day.'" Thus Shaykh Emin's practice of *salāt ad-duḥā* is not only the fulfillment of a noble *sunna* of Muhammad (may God's praise and peace be upon him), but a daily demonstration of this *sunna* as the completion and fulfillment of the path given to all prophets and prescribed for all humanity.

10 Here, the expression *a necessary obligation* refers to the Arabic word *fard*, meaning a religious requirement established by the proof-texts of Islam without doubt or ambiguity. The believer is rewarded by God for fulfilling such an obligation,

and punished for its omission. It is in this sense, derived from the science of Islamic legal interpretation [*fiqh*], in which the action is necessary, and not in the more typical sense of everyday usage.

11 The Arabic term for this as a category within *fiqh* is *mandūbāt*. This refers to those actions for which the believer is rewarded for their performance, but not punished for their omission.

12 The phrase *in each moment* emphasizes the flexibility of the sacred law of Islām. For instance, it is deemed preferable for us to break a fast when invited by our friends to share a meal, provided the fast was voluntary – a point also exemplified above in the biography of Shaykh Emin. In the moment of invitation, our courtesy to a friend supercedes the necessity of fulfilling our intention to fast, which can be completed later. This also helps us to avoid the sanctimonious religiosity that is so off-putting to those who wish to believe but find religious people unbearable. In breaking the fast on this occasion, we do not place ourselves above the bonds of friendship, and we do not tell the one who invites us what we have done in order to accept his offer.

13 The Qur'ān refers to the ideal community of believers as *ummat al-wasat*, people of moderation. An example of a Qur'ānic verse reflecting the ideal of a balanced life is the following:

> *And do not recite too loudly in your prayers, or too quietly, but seek the way in between.* [al-Isrā 17:110]

14 Some readers may be familiar with the technical terms given in this section. In the original Arabic, these are:

- Religion: *dīn*
- Faith: *īmān*
- School: *madhhab*
- Law: *sharīʿa*
- Way: *tarīqa*
- Realization: *haqīqa*

• Purification of the Heart: *tasawwuf*
• Virtue: *iḥsān*

15 A *school* can most profitably be understood as a *community of interpretation*, or a *hermeneutical tradition*. The sources of religious law and tradition require interpretation according to particular methodologies and assumptions that not just any person is qualified to understand and implement. A *qualified scholar* is a person who has been properly and extensively trained in the sources and methods of a school, and explicitly authorized to teach others. The requirements for this are extremely rigorous, and accordingly, consideration of those authorities whom we are to trust is not a matter of small importance.

16 The testimony of faith is the *shahāda*, one of the Five Pillars of Islam. This testimony is necessary for one to enter Islam but it is not, as the author points out here, sufficient to win God's Pleasure.

17 This chapter is called, in Arabic, *Sūrat al-ʿAsr*. The title cannot really be translated. As for the content, no rendering of the Qur'ān can really be considered a translation – the Qur'ān is considered by believers to be inimitable, and therefore any effort to convey its meanings in some language other than the original is really more of a commentary. The versions given throughout this treatise are based substantially on the very fine effort of A. Nooruddeen Durkee, *The Tajwīdī Qur'ān* (an-Noor Educational Foundation, Charlottesville, Virginia, 2003). When we cite a verse of the Qur'ān, we do so in this format: *al-Baqara* 2: 255 (where *al-Baqara* is the name of the chapter in Arabic, 2 is the number of the chapter, and 255 is the number of the verse).

18 A narrative in this sense is known as a *ḥadīth*, that is, something said or done by the Prophet Muhammad, may God bless him and grant him peace, that was accurately passed on and written down according to the testimony of reliable witnesses. This is therefore analogous to the four Gospels of the New Testament, although far more is known about the chains of transmission of the *ḥadīth*s than of the Gospels. (The Gospels would count as extremely weak, defective, and

problematic *hadīth*s of Jesus, peace be upon him.) This is not
to say that Jesus, peace be upon him, did not receive a book,
called the *Injīl*. He did. But, unlike the Qur'ān, this book was
not preserved by the community of Jesus, peace be upon him,
in the form in which it was actually sent down.

A *hadīth* is not something recorded in the Qur'ān, which consists instead of God's own words rather than those ascribed
to His Prophet. The narrative reproduced here is the famous
"Hadith of Jibril" or "Gabriel Hadith" that believers accept as
a particularly concise and authoritative statement of the basic
tenets of Islam. This name is used because the stranger in this
narrative turns out to be the angel Jibrīl, the intermediary between God and His Messenger, may God bless him and grant
him peace, who conveys the Qur'ān to humankind.

19 Islamic religious treatises often employ sophisticated
grammatical analyses that work to bring into the foreground
of our awareness dimensions of meaning and implication that
we might otherwise neglect. (This is, in part, a reflection of
the conviction that the language in which the Qur'ān was
revealed is no mere vehicle, but integral to our understanding
of the divine speech and discourse, the *kalām Allāh* that is the
Qur'ān.) Here the author points out that the noun *īmān* is
related to a verb that uses a preposition (in Arabic, *bi-*) to
designate an object of *īmān*. This is not a minor point, since
it proposes that faith is an action and state of purposeful
engagement in the world rather than merely a passive state.

20 The expression *awareness of the Divine Presence* refers to the
Arabic term *taqwā'*, at once untranslatable and essential to
an understanding of *īmān* as explained here. Other ways of
conveying this are *godwariness* or *godconsciousness*, both of which
are unnatural in English but nevertheless capture the sense
in which the ongoing engagement in and commitment to
faith can be understood and undertaken in Islām as a path of
refinement of consciousness and character.

21 It should be clear to the reader that the use of the masculine personal pronoun *He* to refer to God reflects grammatical

gender only, and implies absolutely nothing about a gendered identity for God. Because God is One, it is not possible to conceive of God as masculine, feminine, or neuter, these being expressions of multiplicity. It is a language that is constrained by sexism – not God, and not Islām as understood and expressed in this treatise.

22 The verb *istawā* in this and several similar verses (e.g., 10: 3, 13: 2, 20: 5, 25: 59, 32: 4, and 57: 4, always with the word *ʿarsh*, discussed below) has sometimes led to needless disagreements among Muslims along doctrinal lines. The author enjoins us here not to invest so much energy in the interpretation of a word like this that we lose sight of the necessary unity of the Muslim community, or of the overall import of these verses. This balanced approach conforms fully to that of the consensus of the scholars of the normative Islamic tradition. For instance, the famous Qur'ān commentary called the *Tafsīr al-Jalālayn* exemplifies this approach in stating that, whatever *istawā* might or might not mean, God Most High will have undertaken it "in a manner befitting Him." And that is enough for us to know.

23 The word *unicity* is a neologism, but a necessary one. English words like *one*, *oneness*, *unique*, and so forth, have lost all evocative force. Furthermore, the word used for this concept in Arabic is applied only to God, suggesting a kind of singularity applicable to God Alone and thus without resemblance or analogy within His creation.

24 Ar. *dhikr Allāh*.

25 In the Qur'ān these are mentioned in *Sūrat Qāf* [50:17] as *al-Mutalaqqiyān*; and in *al-Infiṭār* [82:10-12] as the *Kirāmān Kātibīn*:

> And truly over you there are guardians, noble recorders who know whatever you do.

26 The Qur'ān makes it clear that its message is perfectly conformable to that given in these earlier books. Muslims may tend to forget this point. For instance:

> Say [to them, O Muhammad]: "I am no innovator from among

the prophets." [al-Ahqāf 46:9]

Nay, but he brought the Truth and confirmed the
messengers [from before him]. [as-Sāfāt 37:37]

27 Given here are the familiar Anglicized names of a number
of Prophets who are also mentioned (albeit not always as
Prophets) in the received text of the Bible. Some have names
that are slightly different in the Arabic of the Qur'ān (e.g.,
Ezekiel is proposed to be equivalent to the Dhūlkifl of the
Qur'ān [Sād 38:48]). Other names are not familiar from
Biblical narratives, for a simple reason demonstrating the
Qur'ān's universality. Whereas all of the Prophets of the
Bible are descended from the Hebrews, the same is not said
of a number of Qur'ānic Prophets – Muhammad, to be sure,
may God bless him and grant him peace, but also Shuʿayb, of
Madyan [vv. 7:84-93, 11:84-94, 26:177-190, and 29:36-7]; Hūd,
sent to the now extinct people of ʿĀd in southern Arabia
[vv. 7:65-72, 11:50-60, and 46:21-25]; and Sālih, sent to the
Thamūd in northern Arabia [vv. 7:73-79, 11:61-66, 26:142-
158, 27:45-53, *et passim*].

28 Ar. *habīb Allāh* and *khalīl Allāh*.

29 Of the biographical sources available in English on the life
of Muhammad, may God bless him and grant him peace, little
emphasis is placed on this aspect of his prophetic career. One
book that meets this purpose, if the reader can locate it, is
the translation by Aisha Bewley of the *Kitāb ash-Shifā* of Qadi
ʿIyad, published under the title *Muhammad, Messenger of Allah.*

30 The questioning angels are named Munkar and Nakīr, and
they ask the deceased in the grave three questions: *Who is your*
Lord? What is your religion? And who is your prophet? The correct
answers, given by the believer, are: *My Lord is God, my religion is*
Islām, and my Prophet is Muhammad, may God bless him and grant him
peace. This trial will be made easy for the believer, whereas the
unbeliever will respond, "I do not know."

The life of the grave is described in harrowing detail by Imām
Ghazālī, who believed the contemplation of death to be a key

step towards personal reform. See his book *The Remembrance of Death and the Afterlife*, translated by Abdal Hakim Murad (Islamic Texts Society, Cambridge, 1989). This book also provides references to, and extracts from, the proof-texts that are the basis for the tenets of faith concerning the afterlife given in this section of Shaykh Emin's treatise.

31 Ar. *qiṣāṣ*. Part of judgment on the Day of Arising is concerned with harms done against others in this life, for which those harmed have the right to expect retribution. Muslims are to be particularly wary of harms done to non-Muslims for which they have not received pardon. This is because a non-Muslim may remain unmoved by the encouragement to renounce retaliation offered in the following verse:

> And We prescribed for them in that [i.e., the Torah]: the life for the life, and the eye for the eye, and the nose for the nose, and the ear for the ear, and the tooth for the tooth, and for wounds – retaliation [qiṣāṣ]. But whoever [gives up their right] as charity, it will be expiated [for past sins]. [al-Māʾida 5:45]

32 Ar. ʿaqīda ahl as-sunna.

33 Ar. kāfir.

34 This refers to the event described in the Qurʾān as follows:

> And [remember] when your Lord took from the children of Adam – from their loins, from their seed – their descendants, and made them testify of themselves, [saying to them] "Am I not your Lord?" They said, "Yes, surely we do bear witness [to that]." This, just in case you might say on the Day of Rising, "We were not aware of this." [al-Aʿrāf 7:172]

35 These are the Isrāʾ and Miʿrāj, described at length in the collections of hadīth and alluded to as well in the Qurʾān [al-Isrāʾ 17:1].

36 This refers to the qalam, or Pen, which is mentioned at several points in the Qurʾān as a means by which God instructs human beings; and the lawḥ, or Tablet, upon which existence is inscribed. These terms were understood by philosophers in the Greek-Islamic tradition as corresponding respectively

to *form* and *substance*. On the other hand, the major dogmatic theologian al-Ashʿarī [d. 935 CE] insisted that these images are not meant to be understood literally and concretely, but instead accepted without elaboration or further inquiry [*bi-lā kayfa*]. The 68th chapter of the Qurʾān is, in any case, called *Sūrat al-Qalam*, on account of the oath taken by the Pen in its opening verse. The Tablet is invoked in *Sūrat al-Burūj* (as the Preserved Tablet, *lawḥ maḥfūz*; see 85:22).

37 The two terms given here as Throne and Footstool are extremely inexact renderings of words used in the Qurʾān. The Throne is *al-ʿarsh*, mentioned in a number of Qurʾānic verses (e.g., 7:54 and 9:129). The Throne is inscribed with the words, "My Mercy outstrips My Wrath" [*inna raḥmatī sabaqat ghaḍabī*], consistent with the following verse:

> God has prescribed for Himself mercy, so that any of you who do evil in ignorance and repent afterwards and correct [their behavior], God is Ever-Forgiving, Ever-Merciful. [al-Anʿām 6:54; cf. 6:12]

The Footstool is *al-kursī*, mentioned in the famous Throne Verse:

> God! There is no deity other than Him, the Ever-Living, the Self-Subsisting. He is taken neither by slumber, nor by sleep. To Him belongs what is in the heavens, and what is on the earth. Who is there to intercede with Him save by His Permission? He knows what is between their hands and what is behind their backs. And they encompass nothing from His Knowledge save what He wills. His Foundation [kursī] is more vast than the heavens and the earth, and He is not fatigued by preserving them. And He is the All-High, the Sublime. [al-Baqara 2:255]

38 Ar. *ahl al-qibla*. The *qibla* is the direction of prayer, facing the Kaʿba in Mecca. The import of this tenet of belief, and of some of those that follow, is to preclude abuse of the declaration of unbelief [*takfīr*] by some Muslims against others, an act that is too common in the present day in a manner having no basis or precedent in the normative creed of *ahl as-sunna*.

39 In other words, one who is of *ahl al-qibla* remains of *ahl al-qibla* in spite of sins. The exception would be if that person

considered the *harām* to be *halāl*.

40 In this statement, *tradition* refers to the *sunna* of the Prophet, may God bless him and grant him peace, and *community* translates the word *umma*.

41 The author's discussion of *istitāʿa*, or the capacity to act, addresses a somewhat abstruse point of doctrine that, for centuries, greatly vexed the foremost systematic theologians [*mutakallimūn*] of Islām. It concerns the possibility that an action can occur at all, given that the only Actor is God, not people; that God does not command people to transgression; and that transgression nevertheless occurs, together with accountability for it. The reader is advised that this matter is interesting, and a necessary one to address in any internally consistent statement of creed [*ʿaqīda*], but not essential to matters of personal direction in seeking to fulfill the divine law and obtain the good pleasure of God Most High. The nature of *istitāʿa* does not, for instance, acquit one of the obligation to offer *salāt*, or diminish the torments of the grave – among our far more immediate concerns. A complete discussion in English of the philosophical background of this problem, together with the solutions proposed by the schools of Ashʿarī and Māturīdī, see H. A. Wolfson, *The Philosophy of the Kalam* (Cambridge: Harvard University Press, 1976), pp. 663-719.

42 This refers to the ten *sahāba* or Companions known as *al-ʿashara al-mubashshira*. There are several *hadīth*s that give their names, and the lists do not always agree. But conventionally the Ten are said to include the first four caliphs (known as the *rāshidūn* or *rightly guided*), namely Abū Bakr as-Siddiq, ʿUmar, ʿUthmān, and ʿAlī, may God be pleased with them all. Also said to be included are:

- Talha ibn ʿUbaydullāh at-Tayyim, an early convert to Islam who heard of the Prophet, may God bless him and grant him peace, through a Christian monk and later saved the Prophet's life at Uhud

- az-Zubayr ibn al-ʿAwwām, cousin of the Prophet, may God bless him and grant him peace, courageous warrior and friend of the destitute

• ʿAbd ar-Raḥmān ibn ʿAwf, emigrant to Abyssinia who had the privilege to lead the Prophet, may God bless him and grant him peace, in salāt and was said by ʿUmar al-Fārūq to be one of those he would choose as his successor in the caliphate

• Saʿd ibn Abī Waqqas was the third person to embrace Islam (such that he was later able to declare, "I spent seven days being one third of Islām"). He was buried after a long life in the cloak he wore at Badr

• Saʿīd ibn Zayd who, with his wife Fātima bint al-Khaṭṭāb, was instrumental in the conversion of his brother-in-law ʿUmar, and courageous and influential in the victory of Muslims in the Battle of Yarmuk

• Abū ʿUbayda ibn al-Jarrāh, said by the Prophet, may God bless him and grant him peace, to be the custodian of his community

43 Ar. *as-salāf as-salihīn*. This is on no account to be confused with the seemingly related terms Salafi and Salafiyya, used in reference to a modernist political group whose ʿaqīda (if it can be called that) is to be rejected as departing fatally from a number of essential tenets of belief accepted in unanimity by the substantial and normative scholarship of *ahl as-sunna*.

44 Ar. *awliyā' Allāh*. These are people referred to in certain contexts as *saints*, albeit without the common implications of this word in Christian usage.

45 The Day of Arising is *yawm al-qiyāma*, and its signs are well known through many sound and reliable *hadīths*. We can assume concerning these signs that we will know them when we see them, and that it will be unnecessary for us to invest much of our time in searching for them. Our own death, which is ever impending, is to be considered a preferable and more urgent preoccupation.

The False Messiah is *ad-dajjāl*. The Beast is *dābbat al-ʿard*, the nature of which is debated at some length. On such matters one might consult the Fifth Ray of Bediüzzaman Said Nursi, available in many translated editions online and in print.

46 This verse can be interpreted into English in a number of ways. The one chosen here gives *way of life* for *dīn*, which could also have been given simply as *religion*. The Arabic root of this word is the verb *dāna/yadūnu*. This is important because the root meaning includes a sense of indebtedness consistent with the teaching that the *dīn* is a transaction under which God Most High has presented the creation to humankind, and then purchased it back, at the cost of our submission to Him [*islām*], in exchange for eternal bliss in the Garden. The word *self-surrender* in the version of the verse just given is *islām*, which can be understood both in a historical sense as a particular set of beliefs sent down to a particular faith community in time, and in the trans-historical sense as that way of life prescribed for all communities in all times. Both senses are contained in this word, demonstrating the tremendous and inimitable polysemy of the Qur'ān which constitutes one of the proofs of its divine origin and one of the miracles of the Prophet, may God bless him and grant him peace.

47 Ar. *salāt*.

48 The term *speculative theology* refers to ʿilm al-kalām. This is the science of addressing religious questions through the methodologies of philosophical speculation. Being a purely intellectual endeavor, *kalām* is not for everyone. The author's point here is that the typical subject matter of *kalām* (identification of the rational ground of the principles of belief) does not necessarily increase faith, certainty, and inclination to virtuous conduct, and may in fact undermine them.

49 This refers to the attempted seduction of Joseph by the wife of Potiphar as related in the Qur'ān [*Yūsuf* 12: 23-34]. In seeking the protection of God, Joseph knows his imperfection, thus does not entirely trust his own ability against the assault of evil but relies fully on God's assistance, after doing his best. It is one of the fruit of virtue – constant mindfulness of God:

O my Lord! Prison is more dear to me than that to which they invite me. And if You do not divert their guile from me, then I may yield to them and I will be one of the ignorant. [*Yūsuf* 12:33]

50 This is one of the foremost scholars in the Islamic tradition, many of whose works have fortunately been translated into English. A towering figure in the jurisprudence of Shāfiʿī school, his book *al-Maqasid* has recently become available in English and should be consulted by readers interested in grounding themselves properly (*Al-Maqasid: Nawawi's Manual of Islam*, trans. Nuh Ha Mim Keller, Beltsville, MD: Amana, revised edition 2002). He is also well known as the compiler of a collection of forty essential *hadīth*s, and of the *Riyād as-Salihīn*. Imām an-Nawawī died in 1277 CE.

51 The "organs" referred to here, as well as below in the main text, are the eyes, ears, tongue, stomach, hands, and feet.

52 Ar. *nasūh*. This choice of words seems to allude to a famous *hadīth*, according to which religion itself is said to be *nasīha*. There is a marvelous and evocative subtlety that emerges from the use of two words based in the same linguistic root (i.e., the Arabic consonants n – s – h). The word *nasīha* means both the seeking and offering of sincere advice and pious counsel, as well as sincerity itself. It is, at one and the same time, reflexive (depending on reciprocal interaction with one's fellows) and intransitive (pertaining to a single person's firm integrity). One means of engaging in *nasīha* is, as the text has already remarked, to frequent our spiritual betters, and to consult them and embrace their advice to us. Here, *nasīha* is practiced with respect to God, returning to Him in consent to and embrace of the divine prescriptions for our lives. This active engagement culminates in our determination to mend our character being made *nasūh*.

53 The difference between backbiting [*ghība*] and talebearing [*namīma*] – precisely stipulated in the law – is as follows: *Backbiting* is slander, meaning the mentioning of something about a person that that person would be displeased to hear. It does not matter whether it is by word or gesture, nor even

that what is said might be true. *Talebearing* is gossiping, in the sense of the quoting of a person's words to some other person with the effect of worsening relations between these people. Numerous *hadīths* proscribe this behavior, as well as several verses of the Qur'ān (e.g., 49:12, 68:11, and 104:1).

54 The Arabic term for this form of unlawful divorce is *zihār*, from the phrase *anti ʿalayya ka-zahrī*, "you are like my mother's back to me." Divorce is carefully regulated in Islamic law in order to protect the rights of both spouses, especially the wife and her personal property and dowry. It is worth noting that this formula need not be so precise, or uttered only in Arabic, for it to be problematic and unjust. For instance, in Turkish one sometimes hears the phrase *anam avradım olsun ki...* ("may my wife be my mother if..."), which might be thought to apply here. It is, in other words, best to give such behavior a very wide berth.

55 More literally, sins of *ihrām*. The *ihrām* is the garment worn by the pilgrim, indicating a special status that proscribes certain acts listed in pp 91-92 in *Al-Maqasid: Nawawi's Manual of Islam*, trans. Nuh Ha Mim Keller, Beltsville, MD: Amana, revised edition 2002.

56 The *heedless* are the *ghāfilūn* or *ahl al-ghafla*, where the word *ghafla* indicates conduct and consciousness that are oblivious to the Divine Presence. A form of its antonym, *taqwā* (*godwariness*), is used in the verse just cited in the main text (concerning those who "guard themselves for God" through righteous conduct and pious awareness).

57 Ar. *taqwā*. There is no satisfactory English equivalent for this word, which connotes a reverential fear of the Divine Presence, a sort of god-consciousness.

58 Ar. *ahwat*. This is the name for an act of worship or a norm of social interaction that conforms to the requirements of *ʿazīma*, translated here as *rigorous observance*. This means that one has chosen to perform a required rite or action in a manner that fulfills the requirements for all four of the normative schools of law [*madhāhib*], thereby relying on a precautionary

path that shuns the dispensations of which the differences among the schools consist.

Thus, for instance, it is permissible according to the Hanafis to touch one's spouse without considering one's lesser ablution [*wuḍū'*] to have been nullified. This is not so for the Shafiʿis. The Hanafi ruling in this matter is less restrictive, and therefore considered a *dispensation* [*rukhsa*]. This dispensation is normative and permissible, but not in agreement with the Shafiʿi ruling, whereas the Shafiʿi ruling (that touching one's spouse does nullify the ablution) suffices, if adhered to, to fulfill the requirement on this issue according to the Hanafis.

In summary, then, the way that is *precautionary* is the way that avoids *dispensations* (without denying them as normative) in favor of seeking the way of *rigorous observance* to the fullest extent possible. To do so is not obligatory and is not to be imposed on others, as it embraces an extremely demanding set of legal constraints.

59 *Axiomatic knowledge* can be acquired through ʿ*aql* or *naql*, that is, through *reason* or *transmission*. An example of *axiomatic knowledge acquired through reason* is that the whole of something is more than half of it, or that something cannot both be and not be at the same time. *Axiomatic knowledge acquired by transmission* includes knowledge of the existence of God, His angels, the Resurrection, the Hereafter, and so forth – realities not inconsistent with reason, but not primarily reached through it, and conveyed instead through the Qur'ān and *hadīths*.

The Arabic phrase translated here as *through definitive textual proof* is *bi-dalīlin qatʿiyīn*, referring to a text yielding only one possible interpretation, or of irreproachable stature.

60 "Know that when certain of the Faithful enter Hell deservedly, God (Exalted is He!) shall through His grace accept the Intercession made on their behalf by the Prophets, the Saints, the Divines and the Righteous. In addition, all those with some standing before God (Exalted is He!) and a goodly relation with Him shall enjoy a right of Intercession on behalf of their families, kinsmen, friends, and acquaintances.

Be zealous, therefore, of acquiring for yourself the rank which will permit you thus to intercede for them. It is achieved by never despising any human creature, for God (Exalted is He!) has hidden sainthood among His bondsmen, and it may well be that the man your eye scorns is one of His Saints. Likewise, never underestimate any transgression, for God (Exalted is He!) has concealed His wrath among the sins which may be committed against Him, and it may well be that the sin which you now commit entails His anger. And never belittle any acts of obedience, for God (Exalted is He!) has hidden His satisfaction among acts of obedience to Him; thus it may be that even if it should constitute no more than a kind word, or a morsel of food, or a good intention, or anything of this nature, that such an act will entail His satisfaction." [Imam Ghazali, *Remembrance of Death and the Afterlife*, pp. 210-211]

61 "Know that the Pool is a great dignity which God has conferred solely upon our Prophet, may God bless him and grant him peace. A description of it is included in the Traditions. It is our hope that God, Exalted is He!, will grant us to know of it in this world and to taste it in the next, for one of its qualities is that 'whoever drinks of it shall never thirst again.'" [Imam Ghazali, *Remembrance of Death and the Afterlife*, p. 217]

62 One must not confuse acts that are praiseworthy but not required with those that actually are required, as some do in emphasizing those parts of worship that seem to them to incline to mystical intuition (but which, according to the divine law, are worthless without having fulfilled one's obligations).

The supererogatory prayers named in this passage are as follows. First, the established *sunna* prayers before and after the prescribed [*fard*] prayers five times each day are collectively known as *as-sunan ar-rātiba*. These are not, as some imagine, in some way optional, though some (called *sunna mu'akkada*) were offered consistently by the Prophet, may God bless him and grant him peace, whereas those called *sunna ghayr mu'akkada* were omitted on occasion and thus can occasionally be missed

by us. The number of cycles of prayer [*rakaᶜāt*] and their type
are summarized as follows:

Time of Prayer	Number of *Fard* cycles	No. of Cycles of *Sunna Mu'akkada*	No. of *Sunna Ghayr Mu'akkada*
Fajr (dawn)	2	2 before *fard*	–
Zuhr (midday)	4	4 before, 2 after *fard*	–
ᶜAsr (afternoon)	4	–	4 before *fard*
Maghrib (sunset)	3	2 after *fard*	–
ᶜIshā (night)	4	2 after *fard*	4 before *fard*

Also mentioned in the passage are:

• the forenoon prayer [*salāt ad-duhā*], consisting of six
rakaᶜāt about 45 minutes after sunrise, and discussed in
a previous note

• *salāt al-awwābīn*, consisting of six *rakaᶜāt* after *salāt al-
maghrib*

• the night vigil [*tahajjud*], done in six or more *rakaᶜāt* in
the last third of the night

63 The word translated here as *lower self* is *nafs*. This is a
technical term of tremendous significance in Islamic spiritual
psychology, which will generally be left in Arabic elsewhere
in this treatise.

64 Ar. *al-Haqq*, which is to say, God Most High.

65 Ar. *sirr*. "The term implies a subtle entity seated in the
body, like the soul. [T]he *sirr*, the hidden awareness, is the
site of the contemplation of God, just as the soul is the site
of love and the heart is the site of spiritual realizations and
understandings. They have said, 'The *sirr* is that part of
you which is ennobled, and the *sirr al-sirr*, the secret of the
secret, is that which has no consciousness of anything but
the Truth.' [T]he *sirr* is more subtle than the soul, and the
soul is nobler than the heart. They say, 'The *sirr* is liberated

from the bondage of the other-than-God, from its fragments and ruins.' The expression *sirr*, secret, designates those states which are guarded and concealed between the servant and the Truth, glory to Him." [Imām al-Qushayrī, *The Risala: Principles of Sufism* (Chicago: Kazi, 2002), p. 110]

66 This is the first of the two great paths of the contemplative life in Islam, moving from the contemplation of the creation to the Creator which it signifies (Ar. *mina-l-'athiri 'ilā-l-mu'athir*). It is also possible to proceed in the other direction (*the path from the Source to the signs*), from a primary intuition of the Creator back to understanding the creation as His creative activity. Much more is said about these paths, below in this treatise, as well as in the accompanying treatise, *Laws of the Heart: An introduction to the Spiritual Path in Islam*.

67 Ar. *al-fudūliyyāt ash-shar'iyya*, addressed by trimming the nails, removing excess hair, and so forth.

68 The expression *essential indigence* is meant to convey the fact that our very being, our own most essential quality, is an unqualified destitution before God with His power and determination of our condition. This is *essential* insofar as our *indigence* is a real trait, inseparable from our being and the design of our creation, unlike all that we imagine of ourselves to the contrary.

69 Ar. *sū'al-khātima*. We know nothing of the state in which we will die, and this ought to be a very powerful inducement to humility.

This evil end can reach us in two ways, of which the first is the more insidious. In the agonies and terrors of death the heart may be overwhelmed by doubt and denial, especially if our *'ibāda*, certainty of faith, were weak during life. The soul may be plucked from us completely in the moment when this condition has overrun us, and all will be lost for eternity. It is also possible that some love of a worldly thing or a pleasure of the life of this world will prevail over the soul, leading us to turn our face back in the direction of the world. And again we will be lost, with the magnitude of the ensuing chastisement descending upon us in proportion to our attachment to the things of the world that we must, in death, leave completely behind. None can help us against this except God Most High, and thus we are to prepare for it through the remembrance of God while our wits and faculties are still sound.

70 Ar. *madhhab ahl as-sunna*. The tenets of faith means ʿaqīda, or a creed compiling the elements of normative belief. The accepted creeds are those of al-Ashʿarī and Maturīdī; the creed of the Muʿtazila is one that has historically been refuted and rejected. In the present day these normative creeds are under attack by Modernists, Salafists, Wahabbis, and others, and their study is much neglected.

71 Because some of the episodes mentioned in the last part of the Fifth Threshold are likely to be unfamiliar to many readers, the historical details are outlined as follows:

1. *The hardships visited upon the Prophet (may Allāh bless him and grant him peace) while summoning the people of Tā'if:*

In consequence of the growing hostility of Quraysh after Abu Talib's death [in 619 CE, about two years before the *hijra*] the Apostle went to Tā'if to seek help from Thaqīf and their defense against his tribe. Also he hoped that they would receive the message which God had given him. He went alone.

Yazīd b. Ziyād told me from Muhammad b. Kaʿb al-Qurazī: "When the Apostle arrived at al-Ta'if he made for a number of Thaqif who were at that time leaders and chiefs, namely three brothers [...]. The Apostle sat with them and invited them to accept Islam and asked them to help him against his opponents at home. One of them swore that he would tear up the covering of the Ka'ba if God had sent him. The other said, "Could not God have found someone better than you to send?" The third said, "By God, don't let me ever speak to you. If you are an apostle from God as you say you are, you are far too important for me to reply to, and if you are lying against God, it is not right that I should speak to you!" So the Apostle got up and went, despairing of getting any good out of Thaqif.

[Those with whom he spoke] stirred up their lots and slaves to insult him and cry after him until a crowd came together and compelled him to take refuge in an orchard.... The louts who had followed him went back, and he made for the shade of a vine and sat there while the two men [already in the orchard] watched him, observing what he had to endure....

When the Apostle reached safety he said, so I am told, "O God, to Thee I complain of my weakness, little resource, and lowliness before men. O Most Merciful, Thou art the Lord of the weak, and Thou art my Lord. To whom wilt Thou confide me? To one afar who will misuse me? Or to an enemy to whom Thou hast given power over me? If Thou art not angry with me I care not. Thy favor is more wide for me. I take refuge in the light of Thy countenance by which the darkness is illumined, and the things of this world and the next are rightly ordered, lest Thy anger descend upon me or Thy wrath light upon me. It is for Thee to be satisfied until Thou art well pleased. There is no power and no might save in Thee."

[from *The Life of Muhammad: A Translation of Ibn Ishaq's Sirat Rasul Allah*, tr. A. Guillaume (Oxford: Oxford University Press 2001), pp. 192-3 (hereafter "Ibn Ishaq")]

Mūsā b. ʿUqba related this similarly ... and added the words, "The people of Taʾif positioned themselves in two lines along his path as and he passed by every time he raised and put down a foot they threw stones at it until his feet began to bleed. His feet streaming with blood, he withdrew and made his way beneath the shade of a palm tree, completely overcome.

[...] It is established in [Bukhari and Muslim] through ʿAbd Allāh b. Wahb, who said [...] "It was related to me ... that ʿĀʾisha ... said to the Messenger of God, may God bless him and grant him peace, 'Has any day been harder for you than that of the battle of Uhud?'

"'He replied, "The worst I suffered from your people was the day [at al-Ta'if]. I wandered off, dazed and depressed, and only came to myself at Qarn al-Tha'ālib. I raised my head and there above me was a cloud. Looking up, I saw Gabriel in it, and he called out to me saying, 'God has heard what your people said to you, and how they rejected you. He has sent to you the angel of the mountain for you to order him to do with them whatever you like.'

"'"Then the angel of the mountain called out to me in greeting and said, 'O Muhammad, God has sent me. God has heard what your people said to you. I am the angel of the mountain; your Lord has sent me to you to order me to do whatever you wish. If you wish, you can bring down the two mountains of Akhshabayn upon them.' The Messenger of God [may Allāh bless him and grant him peace] replied, 'I hope that God will bring forth from their loins those who will worship God and associate no other god or person with Him.'"'" [Ibn Ishaq, pp. 143-4.]

2. *the endurance of Bilāl and ʿAmmār and others like them from those who emigrated in the path of seeking to affirm the Oneness of the Most High:*

Bilāl, who was afterwards freed by Abū Bakr but at that time belonged to one of B. Jumah, being slave born, was a faithful Muslim, pure of heart. [His owner] used to bring him out at the hottest part of the day and throw him on his back in the open valley and have a great rock put on his chest; then he would say to him, "You will stay here till you die, or deny Muhammad and worship Al-Lāt and al-'Uzzā." [Bilāl, may Allah be pleased with him] used to say while he was enduring this, "One, one!"

[...] One day Abū Bakr passed by while they were thus ill-treating him, for his house was among this clan. He said to Umayya, "Have you no fear of God that you treat this poor fellow like this? How long is it to go on?" He replied, "You are the one who corrupted him, so save him from his plight that you see." "I will do so," said Abu Bakr; "I have got a black slave, tougher and stronger than he, who is a heathen. I will exchange him for Bilāl." The transaction was carried out, and Abu Bakr took him and freed him.

Before he migrated to Medina, he freed six slaves in Islam, Bilāl being the seventh…. [Ibn Ishaq, pp. 143-4]

Banū Makhzūm used to set ʿAmmār b. Yāsir and his father and mother, all of whom had become Muslims, outside at heat of noon, torturing them with the hot ground of Mecca. The Messenger of God [may Allāh bless him and grant him peace] would pass by them and say to them, as I have heard, "Be patient, O family of Yāsir; you are destined for paradise." [Tafsīr Ibn Kathīr, I:358]

[Note that ʿAmmār and his mother Sumayya were among the first seven people (together with Rasūlullāh, may Allāh bless him and grant him peace, and Abū Bakr, may Allāh be pleased with him, and Bilāl) to accept Islam. Sumayya was killed by Abū Jahl, who ran her through with a spear, making her the first martyr in Islam. Yāsir also died under torture. ʿAmmār was also among those who courageously persisted in the expedition of Tabūk, described below. Tirmidhi preserves a *hadith* that reports that "Paradise longs for three: Ali, Ammār, and Salman."]

3. *Their endurance of hardship and hunger during the digging of the Trench around Medina:*

This took place in Shawwāl, 5 AH. […] A number of Jews who had formed a party against the Apostle … went to Quraysh at Mecca and invited them to join in an attack on the Apostle so that they might get rid of him altogether. [Quraysh] responded gladly to their invitation to fight the Apostle, and they assembled and made their preparations. […]

When the Apostle heard of their intention he drew a trench about Medina and worked at it himself encouraging the Muslims with the hope of reward in heaven. The Muslims worked very hard with him, but the disaffected held back from them and began to hide their real object by working slackly and by stealing away to their families without the Apostle's permission or knowledge. A Muslim who had to attend to an urgent matter would ask the Apostle's permission to go and would get it, and when he had carried out his business he would return to the work he had left because of his desire to do what was right and respect for the same. So God sent down concerning those believers:

They are only the believers who believe in God and His Apostle and when they are with him on a common work do not go away without asking his permission. Those who ask thy permission are those who believe in God and His Apostle. And if they ask thy permission in some business of theirs, give leave to whom thou wilt of them and ask God's pardon for them. God is Forgiving, Merciful. [an-Nūr 24:62]

This passage came down concerning those Muslims who desired the good and respected it, and obeyed God and His Apostle. [Ibn Ishaq, pp. 450-1]

4. The endurance of thirst by Khālid ibn al-Walīd and those with him when they returned from Iraq to Syria, bringing assistance to the fighters there:

[This alludes to campaigns after the death of Rasūlullāh, may (God) bless him and grant him peace, waged by Khalid during the *khilāfa* of Abu Bakr, may Allāh be pleased with him. Khalid had been an idolator of Quraysh who fought against the Muslims at Badr, Uhud, and the Trench. He entered Islam shortly before the conquest of Mecca. A fearsome fighter, Khalid fought against numerous groups of apostates and idolators in Arabia, Iraq, and Syria, collecting the first *jizya* in Islam. On one of these campaigns, he and his men drank the blood of their camels in lieu of water in order to persist in crossing the desert.]

5. *Their endurance of suffering due to the lack of mounts, food and water and the like, in their passage to Tabūk to engage the Byzantines:*

The Apostle ordered his companions to prepare to raid the Byzantines at a time when men were hard pressed; the heat was oppressive and there was a drought; fruit was ripe, shade was eagerly sought, and the men wanted to stay in the shade with their fruit and disliked traveling at that season. [...]

The disaffected said to one another, "Don't go forth in the heat," disliking strenuous war, doubting the truth and creating misgivings about the Apostle. So God sent down concerning them:

> And they said: Go not forth in the heat. Say: The Fire of Hell is hotter did they but understand. Let them laugh a little and let them weep much as a reward for what they were earning. [Ibrāhīm 14:19]

The Apostle went forward energetically with his preparations and ordered the men to get ready with all speed. He urged the men of means to help in providing money and mounts for God's work. The wealthy men provided mounts and stored up a reward with God. 'Uthmān b. 'Affān spent a larger sum than any had ever done.

The seven Muslims known as The Weepers ... came to the Apostle and asked him to provide them with mounts for they were without means. [...] He said that he had no mount to give them and they turned back, their eyes flowing with tears for grief that they had not the wherewithal to meet the expense of the raid.

[...] Abū Khaythama returned to his family [from abroad] on a hot day some days after the Apostle had set out. He found two wives of his in the huts in his garden. Each had sprinkled her hut and cooled it with water and got ready food for him. When he arrived he stood at the door of the hut and looked at his wives and what they had done for him and said: "The Apostle is out in the sun and the wind and the heat and Abū Khaythama is in a cool shade, food prepared for him, resting in his property with a fair woman. This is not just. By God, I will not enter either of your huts, but join the Apostle. So get some food ready for me." They did so and he went to his camel and saddled it and went out in search of the Apostle until he overtook him in Tabūk. [...]

When the Apostle passed al-Hijr he stopped, and the men got water from its well. When they went the Apostle said, "Do not drink any of its water nor use it for ablutions. If you have used any of it for dough, feed it to the camels and eat none of it. Let none of you go out at night alone but take a companion." The men did as they were told except two of them ... [of whom] one went out to relieve himself and the other to look for a camel of his. The first was half choked on his way, and the second was carried away by a wind which cast him on the two mountains of Tayyi'. The Apostle was told of this and reminded the men that he had forbidden them to go out alone. Then he prayed for the man who was choked on the way and he recovered; the other man was brought to the Apostle in Medina by a man of Tayyi'. [...]

In the morning when the men had no water they complained to the Apostle, so he prayed, and God sent a cloud, and so much rain fell that they were satisfied and carried away all the water they needed. [...]

Then the Apostle continued his journey and men began to drop behind. When the Apostle was told that so-and-so had dropped behind he said, "Let him be; for if there is any good in him God will join him to you; if not God has rid you of him." Finally it was reported that Abū Dharr had dropped behind and his camel had delayed him. The apostle said the same words. Abū Dharr waited on his camel and when it walked slowly with him he took his gear and loaded it on his back and went off walking in the track of the Apostle. The Apostle stopped at one of his halting-places when a man called his attention to someone walking on the way alone. The Apostle said that he hoped it was Abū Dharr, and when the people had looked carefully they said that it was he. The Apostle said, "God have mercy on Abū Dharr. He walks alone, and he will die alone and be raised alone." [The year was 9 AH/631 CE.] [Ibn Ishaq pp. 602 ff]